Praise for Sla

"Slavenka Drakulić is a journalist and writer whose voice belongs to the world." —Gloria Steinem

"Insightful . . . [*Café Europa*] not only helps to illuminate the political and social problems facing much of Eastern Europe, but also sheds new light on the daily life of its residents, their emotional habits, fears and dreams." —*The New York Times*

"Slavenka Drakulić is a writer of great sensitivity, intelligence, and grace." —Alice Walker

"Drakulić is a perceptive and amusing social critic, with a wonderful eye for detail." —*The Washington Post*

"[*Café Europa* is] profound and often bitingly funny . . . you'll never think about capitalism, modern history, or your perfect, white, American teeth in the same way again." —*Elle*

"A formidable writer." —*The Sunday Times* (U.K.)

"[*A Guided Tour Through the Museum of Communism*] beautifully renders the dilemmas of life under communism as sharp instances of moral tragedy and poignant examples of the limits of self-knowledge. Literature here is an aide-mémoire, not just of the historical experience, but of why we choose to forget."

—Timothy Snyder, author of *On Tyranny*

PENGUIN BOOKS

CAFÉ EUROPA REVISITED

Slavenka Drakulić was born in Croatia in 1949. The author of fifteen works of nonfiction and novels, including *Café Europa: Life After Communism* and *A Guided Tour Through the Museum of Communism*, she has written for *The New York Times*, *The Nation*, *The New Republic* and numerous publications around the world.

Café Europa Revisited

How to Survive Post-Communism

Slavenka Drakulić

PENGUIN
BOOKS

PENGUIN BOOKS

An imprint of Penguin Random House LLC

penguinrandomhouse.com

The essays "The Tune of the Future" (2012), "Once Upon a Time in 1989" (2017), and "Fueling Fear" (2018) were previously published, in different form, in *Eurozine*.

Letter on pages 73–74 is reprinted courtesy of Samuel Abraham.

LIBRARY OF CONGRESS CATALOGING-IN-PUBLICATION DATA

Names: Drakulić, Slavenka, 1949– author.

Title: Café Europa revisited : how to survive post-communism / Slavenka Drakulić.

Description: New York : Penguin Books, [2021]

Identifiers: LCCN 2020026926 (print) | LCCN 2020026927 (ebook) | ISBN 9780143134176 (paperback) | ISBN 9780525505914 (ebook)

Subjects: LCSH: Post-communism—Europe, Eastern. | Europe, Eastern—Social conditions—1989– | Europe, Eastern—Politics and government—1989–

Classification: LCC HN380.7.A8 D73 2021 (print) | LCC HN380.7.A8 (ebook) | DDC 306.0947—dc23

LC record available at https://lccn.loc.gov/2020026926

LC ebook record available at https://lccn.loc.gov/2020026927

Printed in the United States of America

1 3 5 7 9 10 8 6 4 2

Set in Fournier MT Pro

Designed by Alexis Farabaugh

For my daughter, Rujana,
with love and gratitude

Contents

*History without memory is impossible, but memory
without history is dangerous.*

TIMOTHY SNYDER, HISTORIAN

*It takes six months to replace a political system, six
years to transform an economic system, and sixty years
to change a society.*

RALF DAHRENDORF, SOCIOLOGIST

Introduction

No changes were foreseen

I wrote my book *Café Europa* in 1996. Back then, I tried to illustrate the new Europe emerging after the entire communist bloc collapsed—suddenly and completely unexpectedly in 1989, a historical earthquake that left us Eastern Europeans in shock, followed by euphoria and childish expectations. Not a patient people, we expected too much too soon. "Europe is not a mother who owes something to her long-neglected children; neither is she a princess one has to court [. . .] Most likely, Europe is what we—countries, peoples, individuals—make of it for ourselves," I wrote apropos these expectations.

On the thirtieth anniversary of the collapse, I revisit "café" Europa to glance inside to see how the former communist world looks now. What are the important marks of the time and could we have anticipated them? Traveling around, I wonder: Do I have any right to write "us" and group together all the former Eastern bloc countries, just when they insist on the differences between them? Are there in fact any of "us" left? And finally, is thirty years a long or a short time when it comes to profound changes in a society?

Let us stick to the metaphor of a café. Like in any café, the first thing you feel when you enter it is the atmosphere. Atmosphere is, of course, immaterial, only a feeling of the place. Thirty, twenty, even ten years ago you would have sensed excitement, hope, good vibrations in the air.

The café or rather *kavana, kavarna, kávéház, kawiarnia*—as this unique Central European institution is called in different languages—used to look a bit shabby, the lights were dimmed, many people smoked. But they had loud voices and smiling faces, the glasses clanged and you could tell that there was a kind of party going on.

Nowadays, as soon as you open the door, the first thing you would notice is that there is new furniture, modern appliances, a lot of light, the coffee is espresso now, and nobody reads old-fashioned newspapers any longer. The café looks designed, more like a bar than an old-fashioned *kavana*. The people look smarter than before too, they are certainly better dressed, but there is less noise. Yet a trained eye can distinguish different groups and different tones, even polite disagreements. Many of the visitors, especially if they are older, complain about the corrupt elites, unfulfilled promises, loss of national identity and loss of job security—as well as the stripping away of illusions. This is how you can recognize that they are Eastern Europeans. Young ones are the same everywhere, they move around in order to get a job and worry mostly about money. The Westerners in the café also had expectations: they believed that once the political and economic system had changed, the post-communist countries would develop fast and the gap within a re-united Europe would soon close—when you look around, you can recognize them by the disappointment on their faces.

Sitting there awhile, you come to understand that what connects people in post-1989 Europe is common values—while what continues to divide them is different histories. Only time alone could ever bridge this gap and thirty years are but a blink.

If someone had told me fifty years ago that I would see communism collapse in my lifetime, I would have probably laughed, albeit bitterly. Living in Eastern Europe, though not in a country within the Soviet bloc but in the former Yugoslavia, my generation could imagine only more of the same—or worse. Back then, George Orwell's anti-utopian novel *1984* was a book we admired because we recognized the Newspeak, control and censorship that he described. We had already surpassed his *Animal Farm*, in which we are all equal but some are more equal than others, as well as the reversal of such values as truth and peace. Seeing the student protests in Paris in May 1968 and the Soviet tanks rolling into Prague in August the same year could only reinforce the differences between political systems and our feeling of hopelessness. No change for the better was foreseen.

Still, since 1989 Europe has changed for the better. Germany is reunified, the transition to democracy has begun in the former communist states, borders have been abolished, freedom and human rights have arrived along with supermarkets full of goods that Eastern Europeans had never seen before. Some former communist states like Poland and Hungary became members of the EU sooner, some like Bulgaria and Romania later. Croatia was the last to join it, in 2013, and some are still waiting. Many call it "returning to Europe." For the first time there was the hope of a better life and, understandably, no change for the worse was foreseen.

The first crack in the perhaps too rosy picture of European unity appeared with the financial crisis of 2008. By 2015, right-wing parties had appeared on the horizon in elections in Denmark, the Netherlands, Italy and Finland. Suddenly there was a lot of public discussion of an *almost* forgotten topic: national identity and the loss of it. It soon became clear that the combination of globalization and the financial crisis had produced a general feeling of anxiety. But the decisive event in the last thirty years came from outside Europe and divided it even more deeply in terms of the reactions to it and political changes that ensued. This was the great and sudden wave of refugees between 2015 and 2016 that swept the continent, the so-called European refugee crisis.

If someone had told me thirty years ago that the European Union would experience another crisis, this time through mass immigration from outside the EU that would almost bring it to the brink of collapse, once again, I would have laughed. We had already survived one major change in 1989; was another to follow?

Within a period of about a year, over two million refugees from Asia and Africa came to Europe, via the Mediterranean Sea and across the border between Turkey and Greece on the Balkan route. After the initial welcome, EU member states changed tactics and some of them—Bulgaria, Hungary, Slovenia—erected razor-wire border fences in Eastern Europe. Not only did Europe close its doors by limiting the number of refugees admitted; it turned out that there was no will even to deal with those already inside. The situation became worse after terrorist attacks in France and Belgium committed by citizens of immigrant parentage occurred. In the course of about two years, the media and especially the populist rhetoric of right-wing party leaders like Marine Le Pen equated refugees with Muslims, potential rapists—and terrorists. In the meantime, an already existing anxiety turned into fear of real and imagined dangers.

Many differences between Western and Eastern Europe that had existed before, but were not spoken about in the interests of unity, resurfaced to play a decisive role. Citizens of the former communist countries, who felt that they had been treated as second-class citizens ever since 1989, finally took the opportunity to oppose what they called the "dictatorship" of the EU. Poland and Hungary, for example, became self-confident enough to refuse to take any refugees at all. With Moscow no longer issuing orders to these countries, they seemed to be less and less in the mood to take commands from Brussels. On February 11, 2018—the day after Viktor Orbán's sweeping electoral victory in Hungary—*The New York Times* ran the headline AS WEST FEARS THE RISE OF AUTOCRATS, HUNGARY SHOWS WHAT'S POSSIBLE.

Xenophobia is changing the European social and political landscape. Once-timid discussions about national identity are now becoming full-fledged nationalism. These sorts of ideas used to travel from west to east; now they are moving in the opposite direction, as if nationalism and Balkanization were no longer the property of Eastern Europe alone. With politics now based on exploiting emotions, the past has become stronger than the present. Brexit and the Catalan movement for independence from Spain are just two cases in point.

The Romanian philosopher Andrei Plesu writes that "the solution is neither deconstructive panic nor the rosy demagogy of a luminous future. Throughout its existence, Europe has been trained to survive, to integrate its fractures, to transform its scars into signs of life." There is, however, a difference between the survival of a united European Union and the survival of a divided and shrunken Union. There are currently signs of both these possibilities and, while revisiting cafés in Europa, like any other observer in my place, I feel a little bit like a fortune-teller reading a palm or looking into a crystal ball, trying to see the future.

In these stories from the European *kavana*, the reader will hear the rare sound of leafing through newspapers and the muffled voices of visitors exchanging stories, opinions and gossip, recalling their travels, reliving memories of time past and planning for the future.

Hopefully, the reader will get a feeling of—well, my view of Europe.

Café Europa
Revisited

Once upon
a Time in 1989

The Berlin Wall had already fallen and the people in Eastern Europe were celebrating the new era without communism. But the news did not seem to concern Romanian dictator Nicolae Ceausescu until the last day he ever addressed his people, December 21, 1989. A close-up on camera caught him at the exact moment when he realized that the tide was turning against him, that people are no longer applauding and cheering, but booing him. His shock and the disbelief I saw in that face will stay with me forever as an iconic picture of the change.

Apparently, people rarely see the big picture or immediately understand the real meaning of events they witness. In the case of the fall of communism, the dominating feeling at the time, it seems to me, was surprise. Joy came only afterward, mixed with a bit of suspicion.

Such fragmented pictures and emotions are deeply deposited in our memory. The whole big earthquake, its causes and consequences, escaped us then only to come back later as history.

Therefore it becomes important how we remember it, if there are discrepancies and gaps, like we know it from the old times.

Indeed, a discrepancy that comes to my mind when remembering 1989 is the one between history and fantasy. There was a certain innocent naïveté sweeping over Eastern Europe, the hope that the fall of communism would be, in some way, a guarantee that we would live happily ever after. The reason I call it innocent is that we really didn't know what to expect, but we knew what we wanted: glitter and glamour, like on the other side, in the West. What else could we think of, but sheer old-fashioned magic, as in a provincial circus performance? Or in fairy tales for that matter. In our perception, what had just happened was nothing but a fairy tale, in which a poor young man, overcoming insurmountable obstacles put in his way by the princess's father, wins her heart and becomes a king himself. What other concept—or, indeed, "narrative," as it is called today—did we know? Democracy was a vague and distant idea, a theory never to be reached in practice. Human rights even more so. And capitalism we understood only as far as supermarkets full of incredible food and unknown trifles took us. That was a reality we could touch and smell, consume, buy, possess—the very measure of our success. Hard work for little money, poverty and jobless people were not part of that parcel.

We had no experience of the new world opening up to us; we had only dreams made of TV images, movies, rumors about freedom of expression, finely wrapped chocolates and the glowing lights of shopping windows in Vienna or Paris.

There is another reason I think we were naive: the belief that such a dramatic change, the collapse of an entire political system, would go smoothly and gently, with few victims and limited conflict. We did not foresee the profound changes that were in the making, including the fact that they were of two kinds: progressive, modern, liberal, tolerant—as well as the opposite. The coin had two sides, on one democracy and freedom, on the other exploitation and poverty. Maybe it was simply easier to believe in the new reality and not question it, to embrace luxury more than democracy, greed more than human rights. Even if our fantasy about "Europe" and all that it meant did not last long.

Underneath the big change, a reaction to it was going on. When the earth trembles under your feet, you look for security in what you know, in what you remember, in what was there before communism collapsed.

But what was actually there to fall back on? Not much, but there were two strong pillars of collective identity: the national and the religious. Even during communism, although suppressed, national identity was preserved in language and culture. And there was religion, in some nations more important, in others less. It was an inseparable part of national identity, although expressed more in the form of tradition and culture than as regular religious practice. Indeed, national identity and religion came to dominate public discourse very soon after 1989—to the surprise of the people and politicians in the West, where nationalism (they believed back then!) belonged to the past and religion was considered a purely private affair. At first, it seemed to them as if the Eastern Europeans were not only coming from a different place, they were coming from another time too.

But that was not the only misunderstanding. The perception of our mind-set or mentality was just as problematic. It is more difficult to explain and hard to pinpoint exactly what this phenomenon is about, but it is vital to understand Eastern Europeans from a psychological point of view. In 1989, most of them had spent a big part of their lives under communism. This experience, common to all, formed their values and perceptions, their habits and expectations—in short, their worldview. It formed a specific kind of mentality—and while a political regime might be changed overnight, that mentality cannot. To alter it takes time; indeed, generations.

In the new post-communist reality, joy was soon accompanied by a feeling of disappointment triggered by growing poverty and the gap between those who made a fortune when state property was privatized and the extremely poor, by corruption, and by a distrust of the political elite as well as of the impermeable EU bureaucracy. No doubt, there were many positive changes, of which access to all sorts of new products was the only one embraced unanimously, just like in the West. Stability was replaced with the mobility of goods, businesses and people. But when you have freedom of movement but no money to travel, that freedom will in the end, in your eyes, be devalued. "Europe" did not live up to our fantasies, because such fantasies could never become reality. Instead, it was accused of neocolonialist exploitation, for creating economic injustice, for the lack of jobs and the democracy deficit or for simply not sending us enough money.

In the meantime, we learned the hard way that we are not the same kind of Europeans, that some are more European than others. Living in the periphery and coming from another time simply make you a second-class European. Like laundry detergents or canned food in our supermarkets: the brand name is the same, but the quality is not. It feels like a slap in the face, but it is also a good metaphor: What more proof of inequality?

But if you take a look at Eastern Europe from the west side, you could see that we are unequal in something else, in pervasiveness of corruption. I found it captured beautifully in a single film from 2016, *Graduation*, by the Romanian director Cristian Mungiu. The main character, Romeo, is a medical doctor in his midforties. He belongs to a generation that believed in the transition and in principles such as truth and decency, that believed that reality can change if we stick to rules, if we ourselves are better people. His idealism fades away, but one hope remains: his daughter, Eliza. She was brought up with high principles, prepared to study and live in Great Britain. She gets a grant, but the fulfillment of his (not her!) dream depends on her passing the final exams. This should just be a formality for such a bright student, but on the very day when the exams start, Eliza becomes the victim of attempted rape, which leaves her traumatized, and she is unable to perform. Realizing that his daughter's future is at stake, Romeo embarks on a long journey of corruption—something he fought against all his life. You can see that corruption permeates every cell of Romanian society, from the school to the police, from the ministry to the hospital and the financial inspectors. Now Romeo is caught in a web and we see how corruption influences him on a very personal level—for without it there is no way for him to reach his aim.

Romania is in the EU, it is a democracy, there is capitalism—yet only on the surface. When you scratch it, the real Romania shows through and it doesn't appear to be much different than it was twenty-five years ago, when party membership and VIP connections were the means of survival and the main currency of corruption. This goes for most other Eastern European societies, really. And it was my generation that couldn't get rid of it. There is corruption in the West too, but there is a difference between the individual cases of corruption in the West and corruption as a system, the way society functions in the East. This hasn't changed, not even in twenty-five years. This film left me with a bitter taste of defeat. Having no hope for change is perhaps the biggest loss of the next generation. No wonder so many are depressed. Others are leaving, some 20 percent of them from Romania alone.

Donald Trump became the president of the United States, Brexit became a reality; the politics of exclusion are becoming mainstream, and nationalism and nativism are on the rise, together with razor-wire fences on the EU's borders and a "great wall" in the United States; support for right-wing parties in France, the Netherlands and even Germany is growing and threatening European unity; the burden of refugees is not being fairly distributed; the war in Ukraine and the Russian annexation of Crimea have created a feeling that Russia has yet again become a real threat to Europe. It seems that the European Union is in danger of falling apart, the member states being unable to agree on and confront a single important issue. We see confusion and feel uncertainty, but we do not get the whole picture. The changes are many and they happen fast; yesterday's explanations are no longer valid.

Only a few years ago, Europe was a quite different place. Today's problems were surely there, but the feeling was different, there was energy in the air. New countries wanted to join the EU, there was a desire to include Ukraine at least in trading, and the EU was still promising peace and security, emanating values to aspire to and possibilities for a better life for everybody.

In my part of Europe, on one level we were trying to adapt and emulate European standards and expectations. However, at the same time we built a psychological defense mechanism of collective identity based on nation and religion. There was not much more there with which we could confront the new situation. In the concept of national identity all the disappointments with the EU were summed up, the frustration coming from our position in the Union, fear of globalization, fear of immigrants who appeared as new, more needy victims, ready to take our place.

We developed something very similar to what Zygmunt Bauman called "Retrotopia," whose main characteristic is the "rehabilitation of the tribal model of community." We turned back to what was before, more imagining than remembering it. Just as more and more people in the West do today. Nostalgia? Yes, if that could be used as a useful means of establishing a defense mechanism by returning to the past when faced with a reality one doesn't understand. However, it is more than that: it is a restorative, antimodern form of nostalgia, a nationalist revival that reached its peak in the Yugoslav wars and currently attracts voters all over Europe and beyond.

The problem was that the concept of national identity was a very old-fashioned one: this identity was perceived as cast in stone, fixed forever—that was exactly why it was perceived as something steady and stable, something secure to fall back on. However, national identity is in reality anything but that. In modern anthropology it is defined as a construct made up of all kinds of material, from history to myths, from folk tales to kings one does not even know for sure existed, as well as symbols contrived much more recently. For example, the newly created state of Croatia had to invent all its basic symbols—from its flag to its national anthem, its uniforms to its honorary medals.

As in most Eastern European countries, one of the defining elements of national identity in the former Yugoslavia, a federal state, had been religion—Roman Catholic, Orthodox and Muslim. Religious practice was not forbidden, but the majority of the population did not practice it (for understandable reasons)—and still it didn't disappear, not from culture, nor from habits and values, national myths and folklore. Or, to formulate it differently, religion was not eradicated by communist propaganda, it went underground. And then it reappeared, rehabilitated, just before and during the wars. Suddenly, culture and national belonging were explicitly connected to religion, and vice versa. This was regardless of whether you were a believer or not—but wars do not allow for such "nuances." To be Croat meant to be Catholic. To be Serb meant to be Orthodox.

As should already be obvious, it is difficult for me not to mention the wars between 1991 and 1995 in the former Yugoslavia. These wars did not fit into the general picture at the time; they were in stark contrast to the peaceful process of unification and transition that characterized other countries. No one in the West could understand what happened back then, and, I am afraid, it's no different today. Moreover, Yugoslavia was the most prosperous and free of the communist countries—in comparison to the Soviet bloc. Was it just an outburst of hatred between belligerent Balkan tribes? Indeed, in the absence of a coherent explanation, many were ready to embrace the old Balkan cliché of "hundreds of years of hatred." But the key was just there: it was exactly the fact that Yugoslavia didn't belong to the bloc that laid the ground for these conflicts. That Yugoslavia had developed its own kind of socialism meant that resistance to authoritarianism was weaker here than in, for example, Czechoslovakia or Poland. In Yugoslavia there was no Václav Havel, Adam Michnik or Lech Wałesa. There was no democratic opposition building up under communist rule—nor against the growing nationalism.

There were, for sure, many political and economic reasons to create tension and form opposition in the Yugoslav federation—

but nobody but the nationalists were politically organized and ready to take over political power, even if it was at the price of going to war. Nationalist leaders were called Slobodan Milošević, Radovan Karadžić, Vojislav Šešelj, Franjo Tuđman and Alija Izetbegović. Yes, Serbia attacked Croatia first, then Bosnia, and Kosovo's status is still not completely resolved. But the point is that some twenty years and 150,000 victims later, independent nation-states found themselves at the doorstep of the European Union. And they were all hoping to join yet another union, ready to renounce their newly won sovereignty in a turnaround that one can only describe as the "Balkan paradox." If there is anything to learn from the wars in the former Yugoslavia, it is that a step back into our own past is always possible.

The wars were ignited by nationalist propaganda. In that propaganda, equating nation with religion, and vice versa, was the main strategy. In prewar propaganda, nation and religion became a means to identify and distinguish the "enemy." Furthermore, it became a means of exclusion. In a culture that for decades had been presumed to be atheist, religion fused with national belonging suddenly became a matter of life and death: Catholic Croats vs. Orthodox Serbs, Orthodox Serbs vs. Muslim Bosnians. . . .

This political use of identity, *reducing a nation to a religion*, was the vanguard of what is happening today in the rest of Europe. Today's immigrants and refugees are, in the same way, no longer allowed to be individuals, not even members of a state or a nation. They are reduced to a religious identity.

Defining identity as something fluid, multilayered and non-monolithic is out—for all of us, but above all for the migrants. They are all reduced to a single quality, to their Muslim religion, regardless of whether they are believers or not. And every Muslim is a terrorist suspect. This practice of reducing individual human beings to their (alleged) religious identity is certainly not limited to Europe; Trump's "Muslim ban" is a product of the same kind of thinking.

We tend to forget that we too are being reduced in the same way. We are all together reduced to the lowest common denominator, to an ugly face of Europe—one we never wanted and couldn't imagine would ever appear again.

European Food Apartheid

Are all stomachs not the same?

One morning at breakfast, while cutting a slice of dark bread and spreading butter on it, I was transported back to the 1950s, to our old kitchen in the former Yugoslavia. I was eating the very same breakfast from childhood, a slice of dark bread and butter with a spoon of jam on top. There wasn't much else to eat back then except three kinds of bread: black, half-white and white. No fancy cornflakes, no croissants or Danish pastries. The whole family drank either coffee made of barley or chicory, with milk, or a cup of so-called black Russian tea. It was while visiting relatives in Italy in the mid-1960s that I tried a chocolate spread called Nutella for the first time; it was the finest thing I had ever tasted. Having it for breakfast was a true feast for me.

This is why, when my friend Marta from Bratislava visited me in Vienna with her six-year-old grandson, Tomasz, I served him Nutella for breakfast. He ate with great gusto, chocolate covering his fingers and a little bit on his nose.

"Grandma," Tomasz said suddenly, "why does chocolate in Vienna taste better than the same one at home?"

To my surprise, Marta nodded.

"You are right," she said. "Many things taste better here because, although they look the same, they *are* better. They are not the same as at home. See this strawberry yogurt from the supermarket here? I think it has more strawberries in it than the same brand of yogurt I buy at home."

But the jars were just the same, he protested, how could the yogurt be different? Tomasz is a curious boy and, having tasted the difference but knowing nothing about food production and distribution in the European Union, he asked the logical question.

This brought us to the heart of a recent controversy about differences between food products in Eastern and Western Europe. The labels are the same but the content is different! Not much different, but still.

This yogurt has 40 percent more strawberries here, Marta explained.

Really? Now it was my turn to be surprised: Are you sure you are not imagining that?

But no, this is not a new thing. Many of us Slovaks, especially from Bratislava, cross the border in order to shop in a nearby town some thirty or forty kilometers away. Not only because of the prices, but because of differences like this. People just sensed that the products were not the same, but now we have proof that they are not identical. Take Iglo fish sticks, one of Tomasz's favorite foods, something that in fact I planned to serve him for dinner. If you buy them here they contain more fish. Of course they will taste better, just like Nescafé, Coca-Cola or Milka chocolate.

I wondered if there was an end to that list.

After people complained to consumer protection agencies or in the local media, various agencies compared the products and discovered considerable differences. Not just in Slovakia, but in other Eastern European countries as well. Just when we believed that we finally have the same as them. Remember how after '89 we visited the first big new supermarket near my apartment together, hardly believing what we saw on the shelves there?

Indeed, I remembered that the supermarket had been a big sensation compared with the small sad neighborhood shops, where it was hard to get bread if you did not get up early enough, and where cabbage and potatoes were just about the only vegetables available. But Slovakia was not that bad, Poland and Bulgaria were much worse off. There, in the late 1980s, the shelves were still lined with jars of pickled vegetables and cans of compote; milk was not easy to find in Sofia. When the very first private supermarket opened in Bucharest in the early 1990s, I watched people walking along the shelves, marveling at the products. But these times are long gone. Now every village has supermarkets full of foreign products, from cheeses to salami, from chocolate to milk products, from fish to fine vegetables wrapped in plastic. Is this not a picture of a consumer paradise that reveals the main reason people hated communism? Back then, imported goods were a form of symbolic confirmation of the successful transition to a capitalist economy. When we entered the EU, we believed it to be a community in which all citizens enjoyed an equal right to freedom; it did not occur to us that Coke and Nutella would not be of the same quality. The fact that there was no money to buy such fine food was less important, at least back then.

Someone once told me that Coca-Cola is sweeter in Slovenia. When I tasted it in order to check, it was really so. Is the company cheating us? I wondered, but dismissed such a thought as paranoid. I remember how we collected the bottles and cans when someone brought Coke from abroad and kept them as decorations. Why would the adored Coca-Cola cheat us? Nescafé somehow tasted better in Vienna too, but perhaps that was a side effect of the city's baroque beauty.

My hairdresser in the small town in Croatia where I spend my summers tried to bring me to my senses. Once a month she drives to the first supermarket across the Italian border for a big shopping trip. It is not so much about saving money, she told me, although many products are cheaper there. It is about the difference in quality, she explained. So I buy everything, from canned tomatoes and frozen food to Coke. But I really go for washing liquids, Ariel and Persil. I have to wash a lot of towels every day and I can tell the difference if I wash them in Ariel produced in Eastern Europe or somewhere in the West.

I did not comment but thought how our people are never satisfied with what they get. Only yesterday they had nothing to buy— and now they are disappointed by a difference in *quality*! It looked as if she and the other people I heard telling such stories were right, but I preferred to live in denial. Admitting that we are second-class consumers would lead me straight in the direction of George Orwell's novel *Animal Farm*, which describes a society in which all members are equal, but some are more equal than others. I would lose my trust in the Union, perhaps in the free market economy too.

First to take action, insisting on research and investigation in 2013, were two EU parliamentarians, Biljana Borzan from Croatia and Olga Sehnalova from the Czech Republic. In 2017, Slovakia's consumer association tested a selection of food from supermarkets in eight EU member states: Germany, Austria, the Czech Republic, Poland, Slovakia, Hungary, Romania and Bulgaria. In some products they found small differences—in any case, the products were not identical—but there were much bigger differences in others. They tasted different and the content was different as well, from Knorr soup to Iglo fish sticks (the latter had 58 percent fish instead of 65 percent). Slovakia's Ministry of Agriculture drew similar conclusions when comparing twenty-two same-brand products bought in Bratislava and in two Austrian towns across the border. Half of them tasted and looked different and had different compositions. For instance, a German orange drink purchased in Bratislava contained no actual juice, unlike the same product sold in Austria, which had some amount of juice.

When other countries followed suit, they found roughly the same differences. Hungary's food safety authority examined twenty-four products sold in both Hungary and Austria. It found, among other things, that the domestic version of Manner wafers was less crunchy (and crunchiness is just about the most important "ingredient" they offer!), and the local Nutella not as creamy as the Austrian one. Little Tomasz was right.

In Poland, Leibniz biscuits contain 5 percent butter and some palm oil, while those sold in the company's home market of Germany contain 12 percent butter and no palm oil, a cheap alternative to butter. The Slovene consumer association examined thirty-two products sold in Slovenia and Austria and identified ten where there was a difference in quality. The point is that the inferior version of the product was always placed in an Eastern European country and never in a Western country.

Slovenian Milka chocolate was, for example, almost the same— but with an additive not present in Austrian Milka chocolate.

However, you would know this only if you bothered to read the ingredients, which very few people do. So nothing is hidden; but who reads small print?

My favorite finding concerns Kotányi pepper. It sounds hilarious, but even pepper is not the same everywhere! You would not think this possible, because all Kotányi pepper is packed in one and the same factory. However, the content was still different in different countries: pepper in Slovakia and Hungary (and Austria!) was more humid than it should be. Pepper in Bulgaria had too many crushed seeds, while paprika contained only 108.9 grams of red pepper extract per kilogram compared to 140 grams per kilogram in the packet for the Austrian market.

Coca-Cola and Nescafé Gold are different too, but at least Nescafé confirmed the differences: "the recipe [. . .] differs in European markets depending on consumer preferences that differ from market to market."

In the midst of all this research and talk about food, I was happy to see that the Czechs did not forget my Croatian hairdresser and her claim about washing liquid, or in this case washing powder. Here, the explanation they got from the producer is worth mentioning: the powder is weaker because Czechs put more of it in the washing machine.

The media reverberated strongly with the results of all this analysis, although it seemed to some pundits that too few sample products were tested and the differences that had been found were too small. That said, the *Frankfurter Allgemeine Zeitung*, a major German daily newspaper, considered the results bad enough to headline their article on the subject PIG FEED FOR EASTERN EUROPEANS? Other media outlets reported on Eastern Europe as being a "European garbage can"—there was no lack of imagination when it came to describing the food situation.

Of course, the companies in question had to defend themselves and try to come up with plausible explanations. This generally boiled down to "catering to local tastes and preferences." The U.K.-based manufacturer of Iglo fish sticks said it adapts the product to local tastes and preferences, which are not the same in Austria and Slovakia, the Czech Republic or Hungary. But this only added insult to injury, suggesting that Slovaks, Czechs, Hungarians, Poles and Croats—or the entire post-communist part of the EU—have bad taste.

What else could producers say? Certainly not the truth, that the reason for all this is that these markets are more cash-strapped and less competitive. The producers sometimes reduce the quantities of the most expensive ingredients to keep food prices affordable and still make a profit. After all, Eastern European consumers make less money than those in the West and the food they get is only a reflection of their purchasing power. According to a report by the European Trade Union Institute, the gap between pay in Poland, Hungary and the Czech Republic on the one hand and Germany on the other was bigger in 2018 than it had been ten years before. This means that Poles, Hungarians and Czechs have less money to spend in supermarkets on Nutella and suchlike—which is what producers are adapting to, not specific tastes in food. But it sounds better to talk about taste. In reality, producers are probably not making geographical or political choices. They could not care less about post-communist countries, transition, etc. Their only concern is profit. If the price of a fish stick is higher, nobody would buy it. The solution: less fish. Therefore, the different content is wrapped, canned or packed and named strictly the same, undoubtedly to make the impression that the content is the very same.

This explains the loss of trust in producers, despite the fact that they are not doing anything against the law. So long as the ingredients are declared, the practice is legal in the European Union. The ethics of such conduct is another matter. A 2018 opinion poll for the Czech Agriculture and Food Inspection Authority found that 88 percent of Czechs were concerned about the difference in food products for Czech and Eastern European markets, while 77 percent rejected the argument that such differences were based on local preferences. In the eyes of the victims, these differences are not only a consequence of the profit-driven logic of the market economy. When producers claim that their food product is adapted to a different taste in food, it is humiliating—it means that they consider Eastern Europeans second-class citizens. If those manufacturers explain their decisions as being linked to a cash-strapped market, it means that they think Eastern European citizens do not deserve better and should be happy with whatever they can get. Western companies have abused the hunger for all things Western that Eastern European citizens experienced after having been deprived of these things for years.

It was not long before political leaders in the region took up the subject. There was an outcry about the injustices committed by the "old" Europe toward its new member states in the East; meetings were held with the European Commission in Brussels, and strict measures demanded. EU Commissioner for Justice, Consumers and Gender Equality Věra Jourová, a Czech, said: "Dual quality of food products of the same brand in the member states is misleading, intolerable and unfair to consumers. I will do my best to stop it." Hungarian Prime Minister Viktor Orbán called the food scandal unethical, while Bulgarian Prime Minister Boyko Borissov went as far as to call it "food apartheid."

The logic of capitalist production was then turned into a political issue. The unequal quality of food offered a good platform for the nationalist populism of Eastern European leaders, who saw their chance to stir up anti-EU feelings. Nothing can provide more wrath or pride than food. The Visegrád Group, or V4, a political alliance of Hungary, Poland, the Czech Republic and Slovakia, briefed the biggest nationalists, who used the test results and opinion polls to demand justice from Brussels and show voters they were defending their interests against EU elites.

The food scandal demonstrated that a sense of belonging to the EU begins in the stomachs of its citizens. And that the strength of unity can be measured against the extent to which there is an equal quality of food. Probably fully aware of this, European Commission President Jean-Claude Juncker understood that the EU needed legislation to deal with the issue. In his 2017 State of the Union speech Juncker said: "I will not accept that in some parts of Europe, people are sold food of lower quality than in other countries, despite the packaging and branding being identical. Slovaks do not deserve less fish in their fish fingers, Hungarians less meat in their meals, Czechs less cacao in their chocolate."

A year later, the European Commission announced that it would prohibit dual quality food across the Union, following complaints and pressure from Central and Eastern European member states.

The "food apartheid" was a hard lesson in inequality, and beyond the immediate economic rationale—higher profits—it had political implications too. However, what we Eastern Europeans are doing to ourselves is not better but worse, and we are doing it for the very same reason: profit. We import bad food like eggs infected with salmonella, old frozen meat, apples that are years old, Chinese honey of low quality, all with *false certification*. The small quantities of food that are domestically produced are much too expensive. This is another division, not between east and west, but between the haves and the have-nots. If it is of any consolation, such division exists on both sides of the former border between the two Europes.

The same applies to the story about the production of "garbage" food that Eastern Europeans produce and sell, cheating not only Western consumers. The latest case of this kind was revealed by reporters from *Superwizjer*, a Polish investigative television program. They recently broadcast a documentary about the killing of sick cows in a Polish slaughterhouse late in 2018. An undercover reporter worked at this abattoir for almost three weeks. It sounds like a true crime story that starts with a tip-off about the illegal slaughter of animals and continues with the secret shooting of sick animals and undercover work on the carcasses to eliminate signs of illness. Although a vegetarian, the reporter, Patryk Szczepaniak, even ate meat in the facility's canteen in order not to blow his cover. The cows were so sick that they could not stand and had to be dragged out of trucks and into the slaughterhouse with ropes.

The same morning that the footage was recorded, a veterinarian—who should have been present throughout according to the rules—signed a declaration confirming the meat to be from healthy animals. After the report was broadcast, the authorities closed down the plant.

Poland is a great exporter of meat; in fact, about 85 percent of Polish beef is exported. It is the seventh largest EU producer of beef, behind Ireland, Spain, Italy, the United Kingdom (before 2020), Germany and France. After this report was broadcast and the alarm raised about food safety concerns, Poland identified 9.5 tons of beef from that slaughterhouse, some 2.5 tons of which was exported to Estonia, Finland, France, Hungary, Lithuania, Portugal, Romania, Spain, Sweden, Germany and Slovakia. One could say that at least the meat did not end up only in Eastern Europe.

When the news about this suspicious Polish meat reached Croatia, the country's Ministry of Agriculture immediately denied that it had imported the product. But only a few weeks later it was established that at least half a ton of the sick-cow meat had found its way to fifty-seven kebab stands before it was withdrawn.

This was not the first time that a slaughterhouse in Poland had been closed down. Experts worry because the illicit food chain is so well organized. This was also proven by an earlier event, the so-called horsemeat scandal. In 2013 Irish food inspectors found horsemeat in frozen beef burgers made by firms in the Irish Republic and the United Kingdom, and sold by a number of British supermarket chains. Many companies across Europe withdrew the frozen burgers after tests indicated that they contained horse DNA. It took some time and effort to discover that the horses had been slaughtered in Romania and then exported as beef. The meat was first sold to a Dutch food trader, then a Cypriot one and then on to various burger producers in the EU.

It is perfectly healthy to eat horsemeat; in both Vienna and Zagreb, I know at least one such a shop selling steaks, sausages and minced meat. But it should also be perfectly normal to know what you are eating. Indeed, it is the consumer's right to know what he is getting for his money. It may be that, for cultural reasons, he does not eat horsemeat; this would be true for many in Britain and Ireland. It may be that he would not mind. But the point is that knowing what it is, he could decide. Otherwise, one would have to wonder what might happen next. Maybe undeclared dog or cat meat. Why? Again, for the very same reason as sick-cow meat or horsemeat: because it is much cheaper.

This horsemeat declared as beef was not about food security, but about food fraud. Lies, cheating, false declarations, etc. turn out to be pretty standard procedure in the food business in Eastern Europe, even if it is only discovered periodically and accidentally. As things stand, the few cases to have hit the headlines can be branded isolated incidents that require no new regulations. After a while these affairs are forgotten, a few people lose their jobs and things go back to "normal." The plants and producers involved in such supply chains are behaving criminally because they can—and they will continue to do so as long as this remains the case. Which is, in fact, the biggest worry. Again, apart from providing a platform for nationalist populism, there are other political implications, from the distrust of veterinarian controls and inspections to the distrust of government ministries and juridical systems, all the way up to elected governments themselves.

Food, in the end, is important to people in more than one way. When mixed with pride, it could turn into an unpleasant, politically disruptive mixture.

A Sulky Girl in Ukraine

What people see or don't see

visited Kyiv for the first time in May of 2014. Ukraine is not a place one would visit habitually, not if you yourself come from Eastern Europe. Somehow, east doesn't gravitate toward east, especially if you can go west. But that winter and spring, the largely unknown country became the most important nation in Europe.

My visit happened right after the battle over pro-European politics there had ended, but the main square, Maidan Nezalezhnosti (Independence Square), still looked like a battlefield, its vast surface covered in garbage, the remnants of barricades, sandbags and makeshift fires with people in camouflage outfits gathered around them. The city administration had a hard time deciding what to do with the square. It is a place of memory, especially because of more than one hundred fatalities, victims of snipers in the alley by the Hotel Ukraine. Sweeping it clean could have been interpreted as erasing the memory of the Euromaidan Revolution, of the uprising in the name of Europe against the powers to be. But it is also the city's largest square, and it couldn't have been left in such a squalid condition.

At the Kyiv-Mohyla university building where I was attending the international conference *Ukraine: Thinking Together*, I talked with students. Young, curious and optimistic, it seemed to me that they had no doubts about their European identity. They looked just like students in Berlin or Milan, they all spoke English and many had traveled abroad. When I spoke to some of them, their expectations reminded me of ours, people from former communist countries before 1989; if only we would go "back to Europe," all our troubles, from dictatorship to shortages of milk and toilet paper, would end. As if this were merely a matter of geography. Discussions during the Euromaidan uprising earlier that year within the European Union about whether or not the EU should more openly take the side of rebels had not discouraged these students; they still saw themselves and their country as part of Europe. It was touching to witness the students' belief that the battle over the destiny of the entire EU would be decided in Ukraine.

But maybe they are right. Maybe in their lifetime Ukraine will accede to the EU—provided that the EU still exists.

On my second visit one year later, Maidan was clean. During subsequent visits, as I became acquainted with this big city, I explored everyday life, the types of bread in the bakeries, the brands of passing cars, street fashion, shops and restaurants. When I was a guest at a Kyiv book fair, it was heartwarming to see a long line of people queueing in the street in front of the old Arsenal building on Sunday morning. Inside, it looked more like a picnic scene with young parents and their children playing, with finger-food stands and bands performing music in the yard. There I discussed the cover for my latest book, which was being translated into Ukrainian, with my editor, Oksana Forostyna, herself a writer. She suggested a photo—a very special photo that had recently prompted a lot of discussion, she said. When it appeared on the screen of her laptop, I instantly knew that this was it, this was the photo I wanted for my cover.

It is the photo of a May Day celebration in Lviv taken in 1968 on a beautiful, bright day. The colors are fading as if bleached or over-exposed, and there is a difference between the sharp foreground and the blurred background.

The foreground is lit by strong sunlight. A girl stands on a patch of grass overlooking a street full of people. Maybe it is a park, judging by the tree next to her. She is about eight years old and is dressed in a simple light blue dress with a white waistcoat over it. This looks like her homemade best Sunday outfit, complete with a pair of cotton tights. The tights don't exactly fit—they're sticking out at the knees and creased around the ankles, probably sliding down because of a badly elasticized waist. Her little shoes are pristine white, proof that she wears them only on special occasions, such as state holidays. Indeed, in the background there is an imposing building, its façade adorned with a red flag and four magnified photos of communist leaders, as well as a slogan written on a red banner. Anyone born in communist times would instantly recognize these typical decorations, seen at any official holiday. Back then, May 1, International Workers' Day, was celebrated as a state holiday. It means that it was yet another chance for more propaganda, from speeches about the extraordinary production results of the planned economy and the workers' unshakable support for the Communist Party to accolades for the political leaders.

The balloons in the girl's hand and the big bow in her hair underline the festive atmosphere. With her brown hair cut short in typical sixties style—straight under the ears, with bangs—she stands there a bit annoyed, as if she has been interrupted in play to pose for a camera. What holds the viewer's gaze is her face, its sulky, slightly angry look behind her state-issued prescription glasses, one of two models available at the time. Oh, how she reminded me of myself at that age, as well as a bow I hated, a pair of glasses I hated even more, a dress that I was not allowed to play in and those irritating tights that just kept sliding down. . . . Looking at that photo of her, I could see myself at the May Day standing lined up along the street with my classmates, holding little red paper flags in our hands that we were supposed to wave at the parade of the brass band, workers, agricultural machines, young sportsmen and soldiers, while loudspeakers were blasting the endless speeches of important comrades. There was no difference between Ukraine, USSR or Yugoslavia in the way of celebrating this holiday. That girl could have been any one of us millions of small girls living in countries under communist regimes, dragged out by our parents who routinely demonstrated their class solidarity and support for the regime. To an innocent viewer the look on the girl's face reveals awkwardness, annoyance or at least discomfort at her situation. Her facial expression, however, could also be interpreted in a broader, more iconic way, as a symbol of a general attitude toward the regime.

Looking at the photo, I knew that I was not an innocent viewer—we all bring our own experience and memory to the picture.

It could have been a family photo that the girl's proud father took with his new camera and a color film imported from abroad. They were very new then; cameras were rare possessions in Eastern Europe. By the end of the seventies, family albums were still displaying small black-and-white photos with white-toothed rims. This is not a family photo, however. A street scene taken by the photographer Ilya Pavlyuk, it is now part of the collection of the

Museum of the History of Photography in Lviv. When it was posted on the museum's website in 2017, it got more than seven thousand likes and five thousand shares. Hundreds of comments were posted within the first few days of its appearance—not a small number for Ukraine. This was surprising enough, but the photo, even if good, might not be so extremely interesting were it not for the tremendous range of different reactions and interpretations it prompted online. It soon became clear that the image holds very different meanings for various people.

At first sight, it is hard for outsiders, for people from another world and a different past, to see what could be so polemical about this ordinary scene, fifty years after it was captured on camera, probably by coincidence. What is so interesting about it? Why did it provoke such reactions on social media? The posts mostly seemed to be banal: "She looks poor, ungroomed, must be bullied by other children," "She must be an orphan!" and "She is dressed too good for an orphan." Very many of them were obviously reactions from the older generation, the one that grew up under communism: "I have the same photo of me!" "I had the same hairdo!" "Oh, those pantyhose with bubbles on the knees!" "I used to be as grumpy as this girl in my old photos!" There are also some reflections like "That's what Soviet life looked like" and "The look in her eyes tells everything about the Soviet system, how can anyone miss that?" Only an experienced observer is able to notice the divisions among these comments, which run roughly along generational lines, but also along class lines, and between those who take a historical perspective and those who do not. But why should these nuances be important today?

Oksana Forostyna told me that the phenomena of mass reactions to the "sulky girl" photo had caught the interest of Oksana

Zabuzhko, one of Ukraine's most popular writers. In November 2017 Zabuzhko wrote an analysis of the posts in her column for Deutsche Welle's Ukrainian news site, convinced these reactions deserved not only an essay, but an entire sociology course. Reading the comments, she realized that the photograph is both a well-captured "moment of sincerity" and important for the story it tells about Ukraine today. The photo captures a scene, an episode that, because it is caught on camera, suddenly becomes "the story." It is just such an ordinary event and ordinary details that open the door to the past. But what is extraordinary about it is that it offers a possibility of different interpretations—and in them one could "read" the state of the "collective mind," as Zabuzhko calls it. She makes a point of the *internalization* of what people are conditioned to see under a system of what she calls "visual totalitarianism." Indeed, many commentators say the girl looks like Arseniy Yatsenyuk or Yulia Tymoshenko or another contemporary politician as a child, because the faces with which this online public is most familiar are not those of TV or movie stars, but of politicians. This is a much more sinister symptom than it may at first seem, Zabuzhko observes. A society in which the most recognizable individuals are not cinema stars, TV presenters and entertainers, but political figures, has internalized politics and ideology to the extent that they become ordinary phenomena that are no longer questioned. It illustrates the degree to which politics dominates their everyday lives and private time, their associations, memories and emotions. "Big Brother does not need to watch you; he is already inside you, like a worm in an apple," writes Zabuzhko.

She also notices the underlying class difference in the tone of the responses. Viewers' comments might seem trivial and even ridiculous when they write about tights, shoes, a bow; but not if they indicate the class reality in a supposedly classless communist society in the former Soviet Union, of which Ukraine was a part when this photo was taken. When viewers write that the girl in the photo looks scruffy, shabby or poor, Zabuzhko explains, it indicates that they belong to the generation brought up on Russian movies and TV shows relaying kitschy visual images of Leonid Brezhnev's USSR. These are the images that Russia sells abroad en masse via its film and TV industry. In the past two decades Russians have created a mass "Soviet nostalgia" industry that pictures the USSR as the lost "golden age."

I imagine that it is hard for the new post-Soviet generation to understand that the girl in the photo is not poor, but one of the privileged ones. Everything that seems easy to come by nowadays to them, like shoes and tights, were in fact difficult to acquire at all before. On the other hand, memory flashbacks of women who were born during Soviet times—the "it's me" effect, as Zabuzhko calls it, which I myself experienced—clearly belong to the previous generation. Like *la petite madeleine* effect of Marcel Proust's cookie dipped in a cup of tea, this photo evokes memories of their own childhood.

But Zabuzhko could also hear the "second voice," a more timid voice, of the group of "real Soviet children of working people," girls from small towns and villages who had dozens of techniques to prevent their cotton tights from slipping down, the experience of which might have given them their first taste of the system of humiliation that was "Soviet-style" socialization. Decades later, upon seeing this photo, they say that according to their experience these tights were a dream, and they had to wear old-fashioned and much more uncomfortable stockings and shoes. In the provinces, they lacked even these, among other really basic things.

Growing up in Yugoslavia in the late fifties, we did not have to wear such tights any longer, we had new kinds fitting better by then. But I do remember that some of my classmates from orphanages did still wear such tights and had to tie an elastic band at the top in order to keep them up.

"I'm rather puzzled about why my generation failed to defend our children against Russian propaganda, it didn't manage at all well when it came to memory transmission on the family level," writes Zabuzhko. *How come you did not tell us anything?* she remembers one young man asking her in the spring of 2014, during confrontations on the Maidan. Zabuzhko concludes that this silence about the past was a "traumatic silence," a classical symptom of shame among victims of violence. "Soviet girls" at the time, mothers and grandmothers now, were silent about politics not only when discussing this photo, but at the kitchen table while bringing up their own kids. Politics was something that happened to them, that was forced upon them, so better forget about it. But of course "while we kept silent, others spoke for us." Zabuzhko's appeal "to learn how to speak for ourselves" is not only a matter of making a decision. You first have to gain a sense of self, of being an individual. For people who were used to being addressed as a mass—comrades, people, workers—this takes time. Therefore, these women's audacious sharing of their humiliation and their reaction to their trauma, even if on social media, is much healthier than the general silence about the period.

The most fascinating thing about these posts is the absence of historical references, a kind of blind spot. Most commentators didn't pay any attention to the building in the background. They even failed to realize that the photo was taken in Lviv. It could have been Donetsk, Leningrad or Vladivostok, viewers would not have noticed any difference. Not only the architecture but also the portraits and the slogan on the building's façade in the background escaped them totally, writes Zabuzhko. Of course, I know from my own experience that if viewers between twenty and thirty years old don't know about May Day celebrations and parades, or any such celebrations in communist times, they surely would not pay any attention to the photos and the banner in the background. They simply don't know about this kind of thing. Nobody told them that, on such occasions, photos or paintings of comrade party leaders were hung in the center of each town, from Moscow to faraway provinces. Their names were mouthed from loudspeakers, so much so that Zabuzhko herself could still list the members of the Politburo from the seventies: "on the rostrum comrades Brezhnev, Andropov, Gorbachev, [Victor] Grishin, Gromyko." Younger viewers did not notice these compulsory decorations, not even as something exotic or archaic. Nor did they express any curiosity about them by asking *What is the meaning of those odd decorations?*

It turns out that the most interesting thing about the comments on the photo is the very failure to recognize its political context.

It is, therefore, something of a paradox that, as if by a whim of history, these "children," the ignorant young generation, were at the center of both the Orange Revolution in 2004 and the Euromaidan uprising in 2014. They had to start learning about the past from scratch, because the battles they were fighting were against the remnants of the old totalitarian regime, the old mentality and old values, I thought.

In the presidential elections in 2004, young people's votes were decisive for the pro-European candidate Viktor Yushchenko who ran against the pro-Russian Viktor Yanukovych. The election results, rigged in favor of Yanukovych, provoked a political crisis and mass street protests, the so-called Orange Revolution, until a second runoff, which Yushchenko won. But in November 2013, when President Yanukovych (who had been voted into office in the meantime) refrained from signing the Association Agreement between Ukraine and the European Union, anti-government street protests followed. This soon led to the fall of the government and Yanukovych's fleeing to Russia. Civil unrest persisted throughout the winter, especially around the Maidan square. Petro Poroshenko, the fattish but allegedly sympathetic chocolate king and local millionaire, became the new president.

Three months of occupying the main city square, sniper shootings and street fights seemed to bring Ukraine to within reach of EU accession for a moment. But when Russian forces annexed Crimea on February 20, 2014, any such hopes collapsed.

The situation was complicated by the fact that political change and the Euromaidan uprising coincided with the struggle for recognition abroad and the building of Ukrainian national identity.

The truth is, Ukraine is still unknown in Europe, which does not have fixed geographical borders, but whose mental ones can be robust. Besides, Russia was always dominant in a political sense as well as in historical narratives. Ukrainians don't have a developed national identity and they were Sovietized more than other nations in the bloc—explains Mykola Riabchuk, a well-known Ukrainian intellectual. They were considered "second-class Russians" in the West. "If it weren't for the weather forecast, Ukraine would not exist on the map of Europe. It is a huge unknown territory between Poland and Russia. The nuclear catastrophe in Chernobyl, Yulia Tymoshenko, the Klitschko brother boxers—what else does Europe recognize as European? Do they know that, for example, Nikolai Gogol was a Ukrainian although he wrote in Russian? In the public imagination he is exclusively a Russian writer," said Riabchuk.

On top of all of this, decommunization continues—that is to say, a battle for the past. "Decommunization" is a very important word that everybody understands even if they do not necessarily agree what it means. In a country where there is no trust in citizens, the past has to be legislated and that process is controlled by the state. Therefore, Ukraine's National Memory Institute drafted four laws that were passed by parliament in April 2015 and make communist, Soviet and Nazi symbols illegal, along with the "public denial of the criminal nature of the Communist totalitarian regime 1917–1991." This is now official policy, a state plan to erase traces of the former regime. For example, there are not only instructions on how to re-write history, but also procedures for removing remnants of the communist past, such as monuments and street names (as already had happened all over the former communist world *without* a special law). The new law is controversial because it rehabilitates former collaborationist organizations as forces for independence.

As decommunization runs parallel with de-Russification, this affects the country's Russian minority, who account for 17.2 percent of the population, and their rights, language and culture. For example, despite the fact that some 30 percent of people declared Russian to be a native language of theirs, Russian is not an official language in Ukraine.

Forostyna, my editor, explains this complicated language situation: "It's not exactly a diaspora. Unlike in the Baltic states, Russophones and the Russian diaspora are not the same . . . most Russian speakers are children and grandchildren of Ukrainian peasants. In this part of the world urbanization equaled Russification during both Russian imperial rule and Soviet times. Most peasants started to speak Russian the day after they arrived in a city. As recently as twenty years ago, speaking Ukrainian in Kyiv and other big cities meant being perceived as a redneck, a second-rate citizen, and this narrative is not unusual even now. That is another long story—the trauma of switching to Russian to enable social climbing, the feeling of being ashamed of one's Ukrainian identity, the hate speech when it comes to Ukrainian language . . . but ethnic identity and language do not define political inclinations and loyalties now."

The question is: How do you make the ghosts of communism disappear by continuing to foster an inherited totalitarian politics and mind-set? Take the decommunization of art as applied to mosaics made in the Soviet era. The photographer Yevhen Nikiforov has traveled around Ukraine for three years photographing mosaics from the period between the 1950s and the 1980s, the era of Soviet modernism. In some one hundred towns and villages he found over a thousand mosaics, some of which do not even display communist symbols like red flags or the hammer and sickle. Yet it seemed to have sufficed that they were made in the Soviet period for them to be neglected. As if everything from Soviet times were bad—including what was good!

The result of his research is presented in a book of two hundred photos, *Decommunized: Ukrainian Soviet Mosaics*, which was published jointly by Ukrainian and German houses. "When we consider the mosaic, it is worth remembering that it was not invented by the communists," his German publisher explained in an interview. "The tradition of mosaics in Ukraine is nearly two thousand years old and is heavily influenced by Byzantine architecture. They experienced a revival in the sixties and seventies during the period of Soviet modernism. They shouldn't be erased from Ukrainian identity today," his publisher said for a Hromadske television broadcast.

But it is of course possible that, by the same token, a Bolshevik monument might be restored in a little faraway town, a remote place where the new laws exist only as a media echo.

Ukraine is not alone in its attempts at lustration or decommunization. Other former communist countries such as Hungary, the Czech Republic, Poland, Slovakia, Romania and Croatia are trying to pursue similar policies, with mixed results. As with some of these other countries, it seems there is hardly any agreement among Ukrainian historians as to how to proceed, in spite of official policy. "No 'laundry' is being done in Ukraine, for a very simple reason: There's not yet a clear vision of 'what to wash,'" Zabuzhko wrote to me recently. "The war with Russia isn't over yet, and attempts to deal with the past are strongly overshadowed by Kremlin interference (both direct and indirect). Under these circumstances everything in Ukrainian politics seems to be a work in progress."

Younger generations have been forced to learn history the hard way, while making it themselves in Maidan street battles. However, that is better than ignorance and indifference, which create belief in half-truths and ideology, the perfect recipe for being easily manipulated.

The photo of a little girl in Lviv could be an ephemeral illustration of the foggy past when girls wore ugly glasses and tights—but it is also a source of insight into the past. In Zabuzhko's reading of reactions to this photo, it becomes clear that besides the shame and the desire to forget the communist past expressed by the older generation, the comments also tell of bewilderment, of disbelief among the young people who, infected by the glamour of Russian TV entertainment programs, cannot even begin to imagine how dreary the past was. The Facebook comments not only were innocent, naive and stupid, but also revealed how repression in the form of silence works.

In a newly democratized Ukraine, the recent past is still delicate ground upon which to walk, not just when it comes to presenting facts but also to various interpretations of these facts. This is why it's hard to tell what the little girl in the photo was angry about, or whether she was angry at all.

When Aunt Angela
Met Donald Trump

*Angela Merkel and
Viktor Orbán on a seesaw*

When I look at German Chancellor Angela Merkel, I cannot help myself. She reminds me of my aunt Maria: plump and a little stooped over, seeming somewhat older than she really is. Not at all striking. Angela looks like a typical Eastern European motherly type, if there is one: protective, helpful, often with a worried expression on her face. Like Maria, she has acquired that mommy look even though she is not a mother. Every time I see her on TV, she seems so familiar to me that her face makes me remember how my auntie took me to a beach or to buy an ice cream; and I like the chancellor because of that. It could almost have been Angela, instead of Maria, accompanying me and my mother to shop for a new dress in NAMA, the People's Magazine, the most elegant shop in Rijeka, our hometown in Croatia , in the late fifties. The women's department was on the ground floor. Women were addressed as comrades—they would not be referred to as ladies for another fifty years! A very modest selection of clothes was on offer but my mother would never buy anything. She would order it from a seamstress instead. Aunt Maria, on the other hand, did not mind shopping in NAMA. In truth, no matter which dress she wore, they all looked the same on her. She did not wear trousers, which were then considered vulgar and not at all elegant. I wonder whether this was because the women who fought in Tito's army wore men's uniforms.

But all this actually happened before Angela Merkel was born in 1954. That said, Angela always dresses in black trousers and a red, blue, green, pink, yellow or sometimes gray jacket—also a kind of uniform really. With a simple haircut that scarcely requires a visit to the hairdresser, next to no makeup and only minimal jewelry that is always in the style of bijouterie, she clearly has no time to devote to her looks in the morning, when hurrying off to work.

There is nothing much to her look, the clothes are straight out of an ordinary East German woman's 1980s wardrobe, purchased in the communist East German version of People's Magazine. It is important for Angela that this kind of appearance does not emanate authority or power and the danger that goes with that. How dangerous could a woman whom you meet at the supermarket or on a bus after work, carrying home a shopping bag with groceries, possibly be? Something that may in fact come to pass if you shop in Berlin near the modest apartment building where Angela lives with her second husband, the scientist Joachim Sauer.

With the looks and bearing of my dear long-gone auntie, it would be hard to guess that Angela Merkel has been a leading political figure in Germany and the European Union for a decade and a half. This is why it was so extraordinary for me to watch my aunt

Maria—that is, Aunt Angela—visiting the U.S. president, Donald Trump, for the first time in 2017.

Trump's behavior was unbelievably rude. It was clear to everybody that he could hardly endure the meeting and that he had to force himself to control his contempt. While the two of them were seated on the same sofa, he moved as far away as possible from the German chancellor, as if she had the plague. Or rather, as if she were a housewife from the small town of Templin (her hometown back in East Germany) who found herself sitting next to him by mistake because his bodyguards let her pass. Throughout, his body language revealed his feelings of frustration. So much so that the chancellor herself seemed to be embarrassed on his behalf. She even smiled at one moment, something that she rarely does. She also tried to talk to him in English—she speaks fairly good English, her mother was an English teacher. But nothing seemed to work. Patiently and tolerantly, stone-faced, she endured the childish behavior of this "leader of the free world" without manners and diplomatic training.

He is not used to having such women around him—women who are ordinary and modest at the same time as being immensely important and powerful. No doubt he assesses women by their looks first, regardless of their position. Considering the effort that American women in politics usually put into their looks in order *not* to look ordinary, Merkel does indeed look very, very non-American. But of course, at some point in their dealings, Trump must have experienced the other, less visible side of Merkel—namely, that she possesses an iron will and determination, is fiercely dedicated to the cause and has a great capacity to determine the course of events and to lead. If there is one downside to her character, it is that no matter how quick and intelligent she is, Angela can be incredibly—on occasion excruciatingly—slow to make decisions. Notwithstanding which, and in spite of her humble disposition, she is very ambitious.

Traits unlike my aunt, whose looks she shares but who did not advance beyond the position of a bank clerk in a local bank.

The basic feeling that one gets about Merkel is one of familiarity—you feel either that you have seen her somewhere before or that you actually know her. In any case, it certainly feels as if she is one of us. This familiarity might be one of the subconscious reasons East German women developed an emotional bond with her, although she never said that she is a feminist. She goes as far as to admit that "we experience disadvantages" as women, perhaps because she grew up in a communist country where women's emancipation was part of the political system, where there was not considered to be any need for feminism of a Western type. After all, even if she and her parents were born in West Germany, they moved to and lived in East Germany when she was born and she grew up there. She "returned" to West Germany only after the Berlin Wall fell, by which time she was thirty-five years old—and therefore a proper Ossi, molded and shaped by communism.

You might think that her looks do not merit so many words—but this is wrong, because her ordinary looks and modest lifestyle are also her political message: I am rational and reliable, they say. With that look, not in spite of it, as well as her calm and almost shy conduct, Merkel succeeds beautifully in projecting a genuine concern for and understanding of common people and their worries, which is one of the reasons Germans call her *Mutti*, or Mum. Of course this is by no means a decisive vote winner. But the fact is that the Germans elected her four times over.

Her political career is nothing short of a miracle: The unknown thirty-five-year-old physicist switched from science to politics and, within just a decade, took over the leadership of the Christian Democratic Union (CDU), the biggest party in what by then was a reunified Germany. With her analytical approach and capacity to organize, she was lucky enough to have caught the eye of politicians, including Chancellor Helmut Kohl, who became her mentor. But when Kohl was implicated in a corruption scandal, Merkel, in an act worthy of Brutus, was the first to publicly call for her mentor's resignation. No wonder Kohl saw it as an act of treason by his "girl," as he used to call her. In 2000, she became the party's leader; in 2005 she became chancellor—the very first female chancellor in Germany. Ever since, she has led the biggest and strongest state in the EU and, at certain points, she has even acted as the de facto leader of the EU itself. It sometimes might look as if she were leading a class full of unruly boys, guiding them with a sure but soft hand, convincing them that she knows better. The miracle is that they believe her.

Merkel's decline is even more interesting than her ascent. She pulled Germany through the financial crisis and Europe-wide protests against financial austerity programs—especially those imposed on Greece, but also those in Spain, Portugal and Italy—demonstrating that she could also be cold and unsentimental. Everything was all right as long as her popularity at home grew along with exports and unemployment decreased. Up until 2016, that is, when her popularity plunged, slowly but surely.

The greater the faith in *Mutti*, the greater the disappointment in her became. How did it come to pass that this rational, careful, caring and competent leader made a decision that changed not only her political career but the political climate in the EU? In 2015

Merkel opened the borders of Germany and, in effect, the EU to a sudden influx of non-European refugees.

It seems that a series of small, banal events gave way to her downfall.

With hindsight, the beginning of the end can be determined quite precisely. Departing from her usual practice, Merkel visited two refugee centers in Berlin in early September 2015. There, many people took selfies with her. Merkel was smiling in all of them. That too was not her usual practice and was therefore interpreted as a big shift in her attitude. In these photos Merkel appeared as a nice, warm, welcoming person. But these visits to refugees could not have been by sheer coincidence, a kind of sudden, spontaneous gesture. Politicians in her position do not leave much to spontaneity. She visited the centers and let the refugees take selfies with her smiling nicely for a reason. The whole operation was principally aimed at Germans. She wanted to fend off the fear of refugees by individualizing them: they are people like us, they have faces and names. They are not a threatening dark mass queueing up at the borders ready to overrun Europe. Her message was: Do not be afraid, we can handle it. Many in the media took her gesture as self-promotion, concluding that it was good that she visited refugees but that her visits would not help them; more help would be needed. But her critics were totally wrong. It was not self-promotion; she was on a refugee-promotion tour.

Nobody, not even Merkel, could have known that these photos would become a kind of invitation to other refugees. The photos of Merkel smiling with (mostly) young men, probably because they were in the majority and more pushy than the women, became just that. They went viral on social networks. At home they became the most powerful advertising tool for refugee-friendly Germany and smiling *Mutter* Angela—as she soon became known, including on the front cover of *Der Spiegel* the same month, which presented her as a latter-day Mother Teresa. *Come here, we will take care of you!*—this is how the selfies were interpreted in Syria, Afghanistan, Libya, Somalia and Pakistan, even if Merkel never actually uttered those words.

Speaking of the role of coincidence in history, this is how innocent photos taken with smartphones contributed to the fall of a powerful politician. If it sounds far-fetched, too bad, because this is when the fall began, together with more and more non-EU immigrants pouring into Turkey and Greece, crossing the Mediterranean to Italy and Spain.

But before that, at the beginning of what was soon referred to as an "invasion," Europe first experienced an unprecedented outpouring of empathy toward refugees. Incidentally, this happened because of another photo. On September 2 of that same fatal year, 2015, the corpse of the Syrian-Kurdish refugee Alan Kurdi was found washed up on a Turkish beach in Bodrum. This single heartbreaking image of a toddler's dead body lying facedown on the sand was viewed by millions of people and became a symbol of the destiny of refugees. As if suddenly wide awake, people rushed to help them in every possible way; they collected clothes, food, money and medicine and distributed these in makeshift camps, while the refugees themselves embarked on trains and buses en route to Germany and Sweden. Word of the welcoming response spread quickly back home, including via smartphones. Now both refugees and immigrants (those not escaping war, but looking for a better life) poured in in even greater numbers and what followed was a chaos that became harder and harder to control, as the obligatory registration demanded by the U.N. and by the EU's Dublin

Regulation became virtually impossible to conduct. These rules require asylum seekers to apply for asylum in the country in which they enter the EU and to stay there—ideally—until their applications are processed. Then the refugees are distributed among the EU member countries. Moreover, in addition to those making their way over the Mediterranean, hundreds of thousands more were crossing Turkey, continuing on the so-called Balkan route through Greece, North Macedonia, Serbia, Croatia, Slovenia and Hungary.

At the height of the chaos at the borders and in nearby towns and villages, public parks and squares, at bus and train stations and makeshift camps everywhere, Merkel famously said, "If Europe fails over the refugee question [. . .] it will not be the Europe that we had imagined." But when at the end of August 2015, Keleti train station in central Budapest was overrun by thousands of refugees and turned into a huge improvised camp, the Hungarian police closed down the station for almost a week and prevented refugees from boarding trains to Austria and Germany. Only after Merkel's intervention were people allowed to continue their journey without being registered. Most of them wanted to go to Germany or northern Europe.

By the end of 2015, close to a million asylum seekers had entered Germany without identity checks. By opening Germany's borders, Merkel had temporarily suspended the rules, angering others who did not want to allow that. In making this decision unilaterally, without consulting other EU leaders, she demonstrated how arrogantly she could behave. However, her benevolence could not last long. As more refugees entered the EU, it looked as if no one was in charge of what now appeared to have become a flood of people. Every government of every country on the way to Germany and

Sweden simply let the refugees pass through to the next country. Moreover, it became clear that the EU had no common plan as to how to end this flood, or what to do with those who had already arrived.

The resistance started in Hungary with the country's Prime Minister Viktor Orbán. To stop the refugees he erected a razor-wire fence at the border with Serbia and Croatia. Others emphatically judged the move to be immoral. Orbán presented it as nothing less than protecting his country's Christian civilization and culture against "Muslim invaders"; it was protection against "the enemy." He was also the first to reject the quota system of distributing refugees—even if only in relatively small numbers—among member states. Soon Poland, Slovakia and the Czech Republic had joined him. The West failed to understand. Why would Eastern Europe reject refugees? Why not show them the same solidarity that the West extended to East Europeans after the collapse of communism in 1989? But the fact is that Eastern Europeans see themselves as the biggest victims—be it of life under communism, or of occupation under the Ottoman and Habsburg empires before that. Indeed, these countries have also suffered occupations, ethnic cleansing, the resettlement of minorities, huge losses of territory. The end result is a desire to have an independent nation-state and a population that is as ethnically homogeneous as possible. Hungarians could scarcely accept living with their own minorities and neighbors, much less people from completely different cultures and parts of the world. That would amount to an existential threat and Orbán exploited this fear.

Then on New Year's Eve 2015 in Cologne and other German

cities, a number of incidents of rape and sexual harassment by men with immigrant Muslim backgrounds took place. These cases were initially covered up by local police for fear of revenge by locals. When the media finally exploded with hysteria, the fear of rape spread on the continent like wildfire. Every immigrant or Muslim became a potential rapist. This was the moment when public opinion in Germany, and elsewhere, started to shift away from Merkel's policy of opening up the borders and toward far-right groups like Patriotic Europeans Against the Islamization of the Occident and Alternative for Germany (known as AfD, its German acronym), then a small but fast-growing movement, but soon a political party with an anti-immigrant platform. Deadly terrorist attacks in Paris, Nice and Brussels also helped turn the tide, despite these not being committed by citizens of France and Belgium, not by refugees (however, the perpetrators were descendants of immigrant parents). These attacks became "proof" that Europe was, much like Orbán proclaimed, under siege. Could some of the 2.3 million refugees who made it to the EU pose a real threat?

No, but their mere presence was enough.

Behind the enormous human drama of the refugees at sea, at the borders, in camps—and behind the machinations in the corridors of power in Brussels too—there was one question: Why did Merkel let the refugees in? Could it be that this tough, decisive and calculating politician suddenly succumbed to her feelings? Or to her "motherly instinct"—because she is after all a woman? Some suggested that she had acted out of genuine sympathy for the suffering of people caught up in wars, draught, famine, that she was a woman overwhelmed by images of small children and babies in makeshift boats, while others said her decision came down to the need for cheap labor. So, was it all due to economic principles or human emotions?

It is hard for anyone to imagine emotions playing a decisive role in Merkel's decision. Perhaps early warnings could be read into some big decisions taken previously in a way that had been largely unexpected, like when she closed down Germany's nuclear plants in response to the nuclear disaster in Fukushima of 2011. Yet clearly she could not have done this without studying the problem, consulting experts and weighing up the options. The decision to open the borders to refugees did not seem transparent enough.

People who know her say that two things might have contributed to her decision: First, her Lutheran upbringing, which had a big influence on her personal moral views. Second, being an Ossi, she could not stand borders, walls and barbed wire.

Merkel herself, like everybody else, was certainly overwhelmed by the horrific condition in which these people found themselves. It was elementary to her that refugees in need should be treated like human beings and not as a threat. But there were too many refugees entering all at once. Merkel's mistake was to let them in without any registration process, practically without any controls. One should say in her favor that registration at the borders of the EU was nigh on impossible because it would have required a lot of personnel and funds, as well as swift and efficient organization. All this was lacking. Soon restrictions were imposed, member states largely closed their borders and some, in spite of previously criticizing Orbán, followed his example by erecting their own razor-wire fences. They also repeated Orbán's words about defending European culture.

Even if the decision to warmly welcome refugees as future

workers was rational, it does not mean that Merkel had no feelings, only that most probably she did not act on her feelings alone. She sustained her Mother Teresa role—that is, her role as mother to the refugees—for little more than a year. Her image as the caring leader did not last much longer because she had to start to reverse her policy. East Germans were particularly angry at Merkel, who was essentially one of their own but showed little concern for her compatriots. She was too busy helping foreigners instead. This became apparent in the results of the 2017 general election, when the far-right AfD won 12.6 percent of the vote, with most of its support coming from eastern Germany.

In an attempt to save her own position, Merkel brokered a deal with Turkey to cut the number of refugees crossing into Europe, in exchange for some three billion euros. By 2016 the number had dropped to 260,000, and it continued to decrease. The Balkan route was closed. She had to accept that the European system of values—solidarity, human rights—was difficult and costly to uphold.

But for all the effort she invested in correcting her policies, it was not enough to keep her in power. Yes, Merkel became a chancellor for the fourth time. But her center-right party recorded its worst result since 1949. In 2018 she relinquished her leadership of the party and announced that she would not run for chancellor again at the end of her term in 2021. Merkel is tiptoeing out of politics.

So, were her looks deceiving?

She was faced with a cruel choice, a symbolic choice between her own "children" and the refugees she had adopted. Not because it was fundamentally out of the question for the EU to absorb these people, but because everything happened so suddenly and because of the levels of unpreparedness and disorder. Her policy was defeated by circumstances, not because of any impulsive or irrational decision on Merkel's part. But the political consequences of her policies—even if they were not exclusively of her own making—are huge. The rift between Eastern and Western members of the EU has opened up again. The differences in approach seem to grow deeper. Nationalism is growing too; the tendencies swirling around Brexit and Orbán's "illiberal democracy" have been reinforced. Damage has been done not only to Germany, which now has a far-right anti-refugee and anti-EU party represented in the Bundestag for the first time, but also to liberal society more generally. France prolonged its state of emergency to two years (2015–17), two years during which the army patrolled the streets; societies across Europe are becoming more and more closed. The most important effect of the so-called refugee crisis is the spread of fear, which, in turn, serves as a platform for the rise of nationalism and spurs on populist leaders. Merkel looks like she may go down in history as a woman responsible for dividing the EU. Could one person be responsible for so many crucial consequences? Generally speaking, perhaps not; but in certain circumstances, evidently yes.

Imagine a seesaw in a playground, with Angela Merkel sitting on one end and Viktor Orbán on the other; when Merkel is down, Orbán is up. There is a strange equilibrium between these two personalities, because with the descent of one, the other rises. The same applies to their policies on refugees. The balance of power started to shift in favor of Orbán as he became the leader of the opposition to the "open door policy" that Merkel had initiated. As it happens, the wave of refugees not only washed up desperate people on the shore, but a new political superstar as well.

Relatively short and stocky, with an expanding belly drawing attention to his neglect of both body and looks (after all, in Eastern Europe it is enough to be a man!), with a chin up in the air and piercing eyes, Orbán knows how to dominate people. If Merkel has the appearance of a housewife, then he is pretty much the image of an Eastern European macho. Try as he might, he dresses badly; his shirts always look too tight and his suits cheap, even though they are surely not. There is something about these Eastern European politicians that, even today, gives them away as being from the East. It is hard to say what, though—whether it's the badly fitting clothes, the neglected looks or their build and facial features.

I cannot say that he looks like my uncle, but I can say I know many like him. Yet beyond the look of a peacock showing off, one has to admit that he has chutzpah. Orbán is not to be intimidated by anybody. Not that this means he is simple, on the contrary. In fact his quick mind and eloquence ultimately stand out above all else as far as his character is concerned. Unbelievably, judging by his press office and the material it disseminates, Orbán seems to be giving at least one long speech or an interview per day. He is well prepared and not boring—which is already saying a lot for a politician. But he is also a very manipulative populist and an authoritarian in the way he exercises power.

What both of these European leaders have in common is the communist past. But what made Merkel different was her religious upbringing. Her parents were born in the West, but her father was a Lutheran priest dispatched to East Germany to preach in a country that was in principle against religion, that—according to Marx—"opium of the people." It is as if Merkel was born into the opposition and nothing she did later on could make up for this "failure." The two of them, born almost ten years apart, are also different because Merkel grew up having close ties to the democratic West Germany, which she often visited as a young girl.

By contrast, Orbán is from a peasant background. Born in 1963 in a village near Budapest, he grew up in a house without running water. I could easily imagine him running free outside, playing soccer and fighting with other boys, like any other kid. Only education, that is his brain and ambition, could get him out of this village life—education served as a great means of social advancement under communism. His opportunism became evident only much later when, for example, although an atheist in his youth, he became a member of the Protestant Reformed Church, in which he then remarried his Catholic wife, Aniko, and baptized his already grown children. This was a premeditated political decision, just like when he switched from representing the enlightened pro-Western elite to representing workers and peasants. Orbán simply realized that he could reach them better if he pretended to be religious.

Was Orbán the best or the worst pupil of the class of post-'89 liberal democracy school? At first, he was the best. He came to public attention in June 1989, before the fall of the Berlin Wall. Then a slim young man, he addressed a huge mass of people gathered on the occasion of the reburial of Imre Nagy, a former prime minister who had been executed by the Soviets after their 1956 occupation of Hungary. Orbán bravely demanded the withdrawal of the USSR's forces from Hungary and free elections. This was the moment when the previously unknown man became Viktor Orbán, a darling of the West, the recipient of a Soros Foundation grant to attend Oxford University, a democratic activist, a founder of Fidesz (Alliance of Young Democrats) in 1988. The one who single-handedly swung that party to the right when he realized that this would give him a better chance of winning elections.

The future prime minister of his own "illiberal democracy" was initially, in the early nineties, loved by the foreign press, by believers in a quick transition to democracy in the former communist countries, by American philanthropists and lovers of exotic birds who hurried to see one of the world's last novelties, the Hungarian opposition leader. A Western press in need of recognizable personalities and ideas was soon cramming Orbán into the same sentence as Lech Wałesa and Václav Havel—uttering the names of the Solidarity activist and the longtime Czech dissident in the same breath as this ambitious young man looking for any opportunity to grab power.

But power is said to change people too. Orbán's is certainly one such story. It seems that one has to have a staunch Lutheran upbringing to avoid this, or at least more than just a few drops of holy water at a late christening.

Orbán's current blend of conservativism, nationalism and authoritarianism is quite the opposite of what one might expect from a former democratic activist and preacher of freedom and human rights. However, as his former friends and collaborators say, it results from sheer opportunism, not ideology. In this respect Orbán is reminiscent of another such character from roughly the same neighborhood, the deceased Serbian politician and alleged war criminal Slobodan Milošević, a communist leader who switched to nationalism in order to retain his grip on power. This took Milošević along the path to war in Croatia and Bosnia, and then to the International Criminal Tribunal for the former Yugoslavia. Even if Orbán knew democracy in theory, he grew up under communist rule and experienced the authoritarian model firsthand; it is to this model that his mind-set remains closest. It was not long before control over banks and the media, together with the curbed independence of the justice system, concentrated power in his hands and those of his cronies. Thus Orbán became a role model for Poland's Kaczynski brothers years later.

The refugee crisis also offered Orbán a great opportunity to climb onto the European stage, and he did not miss a beat. The quota system and the defense of European Christian values turned out to be the ideal core topics at home and abroad. He figuratively pushed the borders everywhere he could and circumstances enabled him to do so without much resistance. In September 2015, when it was still as hot as hell, exhausted refugees who had already crossed Turkey, Greece, North Macedonia and Serbia were stopped at the Hungarian border. TV screens all over the world transmitted unforgettable images of the razor-wire fence at the border and units of soldiers, with a mass of humans looming in the background. This was the new reality and people struggled to absorb it; shock, disbelief, confusion and outcry against Orbán ensued. In Europe, barbed wire stands for the Nazi concentration camps of World War II.

A leader of a small Eastern European country dared to oppose Merkel and her policy of welcoming refugees. He erected the fences of his own accord, without consulting other politicians or EU institutions, Merkel included, even though he was aware that the refugees were heading toward Germany. Bulgaria had already long since installed a fence on the border with Greece, but this particular moment proved to be so memorable because up until this point, Eastern European politicians had merely listened to Brussels without protest. Very much aware of where the power and money lie, they were not generally in a position to influence big decisions. But Orbán challenged the quotas knowing that he could hardly be punished by the EU. People like him, bellicose types capable of acting on their own, were simply never dreamt of by the authors of all those EU documents and agreements, contracts and protocols. Clearly Orbán saw another political opportunity in this fact. His instinct told him to grab it, because it was evident that in such circumstances there was no consensus on how to deal with refugees among the EU member states. He knew that his fence-building activities would be judged as abominable at first, but what could the EU do against them?

His end of the seesaw was visibly rising.

The difference in solidarity between the former communist countries and the Western ones created the standoff. Orbán defended his decision, sensing that all autocrats as well as all the right-wing party leaders in the West would stand behind him. The language he used to defend his move openly catered to the right-wing politics of rising insecurity, anxiety and fear; meanwhile he presented himself as a savior.

The EU scene is one thing, but Orbán's power base in Hungary is quite another. As elections approached in 2017, he decided to throw a further ingredient into the mix of defending the nation and protecting Europe from the barbarians at the border. Here we come to another characteristic that both Orbán and Merkel share: They both betrayed their mentors. Merkel succeeded in preventing Helmut Kohl from running as chancellor. Orbán "rewarded" George Soros in a similar manner for the grant that had provided him with a springboard for his later political engagement and for the money that the American billionaire and philanthropist poured into Hungary.

Since awarding that grant, Soros has devoted substantial funds to former communist countries by financing NGOs (non-governmental organizations) facilitating the development of democracy. He has spent a good deal of money on his native Hungary in the process. Orbán knew that the heroic defense of Hungary against refugees would soon be forgotten once the country stopped receiving them, so he launched an anti-Soros campaign. Soros was said to be behind the invasion of the EU by Muslim refugees. It was Soros who, together with Brussels, was planning to undermine European Christian culture and identity. Of course, Orbán never offered any explanation or proof as to why Soros would devise such a devious plan—except the obvious one: that he is a Jew. Although Orbán never stated that either. Inevitably, this anti-Soros campaign had a strong anti-Semitic undertone. The tactic worked and Orbán won the elections. He has also essentially forced Central European University, funded by Soros since 1991, out of Hungary. The institution has moved to Vienna. There it could come in handy as a fig leaf to help cover up the excesses of the right-wing government of Austrian Chancellor Sebastian Kurz.

Orbán succeeded in amalgamating anti-Semitic, anti-EU and anti-refugee propaganda into one ugly package. This helped him to assert himself in the EU, with the rest of the Visegrád leaders in Poland, the Czech Republic and Slovakia rallying behind him, along with Chancellor Kurz, Italian Interior Minister Matteo Salvini and other right-wing populist leaders from Sweden to France.

Those who know Orbán well describe his chameleon-like metamorphosis from liberal to nationalist-populist and his ability to tell the public what it wants to hear in order for them to deliver him into power. Neither anti-Semite nor racist, neither religious nor conservative—he is just cynical enough to use ideology however he sees fit. He calls his type of government illiberal democracy: democratic in form, but certainly illiberal in the way that power is executed. But what is it about him that appeals to the people who believe in him and vote for him? Is it his ability as an orator? Or the promises he gives? His imposing personality and manner of address, as if he and he alone knows best? While all this helps, there is another component that matters even more. It seems that it is less important *how* he says something, or even *what* he says, than the fact that he says it at all. People, which is to say the electorate, see Orbán as the leader who tells them what to do, who knows what is good for them. This is as much about his authoritarian mind-set as it is about theirs. They *want* someone telling them what they should do and what is good for them.

Indeed, much research and many opinion polls since 1989 have shown that the public's commitment to representative democracy is low in Eastern Europe, and that, accordingly, approval for firm leadership is strong there. Democratic procedures are unfamiliar and complicated, citizens have to listen, think, choose. Besides, the other side of freedom is responsibility. If a government is bad, you as a citizen become responsible for that. Given the long tradition of totalitarianism, no wonder most people want a strong leader to tell them what to choose. Moreover, the brief experience of democracy in Eastern Europe is linked to corruption, insecurity and the impoverishment of many. Orbán understands this perfectly well. So it is no matter that he changes ideologies like shirts, regardless of how they fit—from oppositionist and leftist, a good Soros student, a model follower of liberal democracy, to populist, rightist autocrat.

Merkel, on the other hand, has traveled a long road from *Mutti*, mother of the nation, to the mother of immigrants to the mother of the AfD, as some call her now. But she has done so without ever switching ideologies, even if she has been forced to pull back when confronted with unexpected pressures. Yet the most important difference between Merkel and Orbán does not lie in their characters or in the fact that both started their political careers in opposition to totalitarianism. It is in their exercise of power.

The success of these two politicians also seems to be related at a symbolic level. As Merkel and her policies lost their shine, Orbán became bold enough to announce his vision of the future: "The generation of 1990 will arrive to European politics: a generation of anti-communist Christians with a national spirit [. . .] Thirty years ago, we thought our future was Europe. Now we are Europe's future."

No one else has influenced the changes to have taken place in Europe over the previous five years or so more than these two very different leaders from two different parts of the continent. Their intertwined political destinies also represent the two faces of today's Europe. But it might very well turn out not to be the Europe that the majority of its citizens had imagined.

Prague 1968: Why Communism Is Like a Wool Sweater

. . . and why remembering victims might be unpleasant

The year 1968 is when I gave birth to my only child. The moment I saw her reddish, squashed little face, which somehow looked old rather than newborn, is not the only one I recall from that eventful year, though it is the happiest.

In the streets of Paris that May, students were burning cars and building barricades. Then their rebellion turned into mass unrest, which the police put down brutally after some two weeks. However, during the night of August 20 something much more dramatic and far-reaching happened for those of us living under communism: the Soviet-led Warsaw Pact forces invaded Czechoslovakia. The country's leadership stood accused of treason against "true communism" on account of its short-lived reforms.

Fifty years later, in August 2018, one would have expected there to be an opportunity for Czechs and Slovaks to close the gap between "official history" and individual memory in their society, a gap that continues to burden every post-communist society. But for this to happen, the Czech government would need to explicitly condemn the role of the former USSR in leading the invasion. Apparently, it was too early for that, and the state commemoration of the invasion turned into something of an embarrassment in Prague. On August 21, 2018, President Miloš Zeman declined to give a speech at all, while Prime Minister Andrej Babiš's speech was received with critical whistles from the crowd that had gathered in the capital to commemorate the fiftieth anniversary of the occupation. Then Czech public television, in an effort to restore some dignity to the event, took the unprecedented decision to broadcast the speech by Slovakia's president, Andrej Kiska, instead. Slovaks probably felt this to be justified because, in 1968, their territory was occupied as well; Czechoslovakia split in two states only in 1993.

This pretty disgraceful incident was barely noticed in the rest of Europe, where it was received as a bizarre piece of news that was devoid of historical context and did not deserve a closer look or any kind of explanation. A terrible heat wave hit Europe, while fear of Muslim refugees and terrorism was spreading like a wildfire; Vladimir Putin attended the wedding of the Austrian minister of foreign affairs—privately, she explained—and the important anniversary simply got lost in media dross.

Was there a desire to forget the event altogether? And if so, why?

Why the Czech government's awkward silence and evident discomfort? It was probably because of the political situation: President Zeman's cozy relations with Putin meant that he feared speaking up and suggesting any association with the occupation of

Crimea in Ukraine, which could provoke mighty Russia's wrath. For Zeman, Crimea was a "fait accompli," as he said when Russian forces invaded the region in 2014. Besides, in a new wave of reinterpretation of the history of communism, Russia claims that the Czechoslovakian leadership asked for assistance from their Soviet brothers in 1968.

As a result, on the fiftieth anniversary of the invasion, the Czech government missed yet another opportunity to set the record straight. Occupying forces left 137 dead and more than 500 injured in their wake. However, half a century later, the Czech people did not seem particularly eager to pay their respects to the victims either. Nor did they grieve much over the destiny of Jan Palach, a symbol of the crushed Prague Spring, who was barely mentioned at the ceremony.

For my generation, 1968 is an emblematic year, one in which we appeared on the world stage in order to change it. We believed that we could fight against wars and racism with peaceful protests and sit-ins, protest songs, philosophy and poetry. Born after World War II, we changed the "spirit of the time" with our counterculture: growing our hair long, wearing colorful clothes and *Make love not war* buttons, making peace signs, singing "We Shall Overcome," meditating with the Beatles and Maharishi Mahesh Yogi, smoking marijuana, experimenting with LSD and eating brown rice. However, it has to be said that most of this took place mainly in the United States and Western Europe. Besides, Americans have very different memories of that time than Western Europeans: while hippies, flower power, Woodstock, Janis Joplin and Bob Dylan are part of collective memory on both sides of the Atlantic, protests against the Vietnam War police beating black students, and the assassinations of Martin Luther King Jr. and Robert Kennedy all happened over there. The protests in Paris, Berlin, Frankfurt and Rome looked different and had very different consequences. In Italy for example, student protests did not receive the mass support they did in Paris, and some groups in the country, and in West Germany too, turned extreme left or terrorist—like the Red Brigades and the Red Army Faction.

That summer, just eleven days before the tanks rolled into the Czechoslovak capital, Yugoslav President Josip Broz Tito made an official visit to Prague. Branded a "revisionist" by the Soviets after he dared to confront Stalin in 1948, Tito was received much too cordially by comrade Alexander Dubček, the first secretary of the Czech Communist Party as of January that year. Dubček, a sympathetic guy, had just begun to make reforms that would chip away at Stalinist socialism and create a more relaxed, democratized society akin to that in Yugoslavia.

My trip to Sweden in 1970, where I would work on a three-month student visa, demonstrated the difference between a country inside the Soviet bloc and one outside it. I traveled via Prague because tickets through communist countries were much cheaper, but we could travel freely to the West too. By then hundreds of thousands of so-called temporary guest workers had left Yugoslavia to work in Germany. The money they saved they sent back home, where the economy was plagued by unemployment. It did not, curiously enough, occur to my generation to ask ourselves why, in order to work, people had to leave the country—yet this fact alone should have smacked of the failure of the whole planned economy project.

Two of the most important Dubček reforms included an end to media censorship and the introduction of free discussion and critique. The entire political landscape was about to change too: there was even talk of re-establishing the forbidden Social Democratic Party for the first time since the one-party system was installed in February 1948. From today's point of view, these reforms look like a premature perestroika of sorts. But the ever watchful Soviets recognized the Western capitalist tendencies in the economy and in this attempt to re-create a multiparty system.

By the time Tito visited, General Secretary of the Soviet Communist Party Leonid Brezhnev had already mobilized the troops. He had no doubt that Czechoslovakia, with its newly introduced social and political reforms, was on its way to "socialism with a human face," and Tito's visit was only further evidence of this. Dubček had to be stopped at all costs. If not, a scenario like the Hungarian revolution of 1956 could reoccur at any time. Back then tanks had rolled into Budapest to crush the uprising of people against the communist regime. The streets were literally covered in the blood and corpses of several thousand Hungarians who had fought fiercely for weeks and lost. Some 200,000 Hungarians fled the country. The Soviet leadership could scarcely forgive the then prime minister Imre Nagy, who took refuge in the Yugoslav embassy after the rebellion was crushed.

The Soviets did not wait for further signs of treason. Better to finish things off sooner rather than later, Brezhnev reasoned, so that others in the Soviet bloc don't get any strange ideas. Budapest in 1956 should have been taken as a warning to Prague in 1968.

Late in the evening of August 20, hundreds of tanks rolled over the Czechoslovakian border in "defense" of communism, together with 300,000 soldiers. Early the next morning Prague citizens heard airplanes, sirens and conflicting news reports on the radio. For a few hours, they were in total confusion until Dubček addressed the nation. He told people to continue with their daily business as civilized citizens faithful to the ideals of communism. With hindsight, it is clear that he wanted to avoid a bloodbath and therefore signed the humiliating protocol about collaboration with the Soviets accordingly. This was capitulation.

Not everybody obeyed Dubček, and for the first few days there were street protests and skirmishes with occupation soldiers; people threw stones and petrol bombs at tanks and risked their lives. There were fatalities on both sides.

A number of black-and-white photos from that time record feelings and behavior that range from innocent curiosity among young people approaching the soldiers and talking to them, to throwing petrol bombs at them or simply ignoring them. You can see anger and dismay on the faces of passersby, you can see fear, even despair, but you can also see defiance as some deliberately pass by a tank oblivious to its presence. I still remember one particular photo: a well-dressed young woman in high heels crossing the street with a tank coming at her from a side street. Astonishingly, she appears to be unaware of the combat vehicle. Yet this was not possible, because the tank was perhaps just fifty meters away from her. She could not have ignored its presence, she could only have pretended not to see it, out of defiance. But most citizens did as they were told, doing nothing but continuing with their daily errands—work, school, shopping—as if tanks and soldiers on the streets were a normal presence. As if they were paralyzed by the mere thought of what could happen if they dared oppose such an enormous show of power.

A few months later, failing to comprehend the degrading behavior of his compatriots, one student set himself on fire.

I visited Prague two years after the occupation. In those days it was a gray, gloomy city that had long since lost its splendor. At first sight, there were no visible traces of recent events. I went to the place on Wenceslas Square where, as I was told by a Czech friend, on January 16, 1969, the nineteen-year-old Jan Palach set himself on fire in protest—or rather, despair at the absence of protest—against the Soviet occupation. It was a pilgrimage of sorts, a gesture of respect to a fellow student of my age. Palach was willing to take on the impossible task of shaking the conscience of an entire country. He believed that there was nothing normal about the occupation.

As I stood there, with my back to the imposing façade of the National Museum, I tried to imagine Palach's state of mind while on his way to the square. By the time he arrived, he probably no longer felt cold or fear; his determination made him concentrate on the act itself. How did it happen? I asked myself, frightened by my own vivid imagination.

It was early afternoon on a chilly winter's day. The square was busy as usual; the dilapidated baroque façades of the houses were silent like the people hurrying by, minding their own business. Palach had chosen a spot in front of the museum. I imagined that he was dressed in his best clothes because he was going to perform a solemn act. Did he have time to look around one more time, to kind of say goodbye to Prague? Did he think of his mother living alone in the house in the town of Všetaty, where he and his brother grew up? Or was it too late to indulge in such sentiments? He probably knew he had to act fast, not only because his behavior could attract police suspicion, but because he would not be able to trust his own responses once the pain seized him. Therefore, he must have quickly poured petrol over his head and shoulders and lit a match with his wet hands.

It is likely that no one paid attention to Jan, not at that moment. Only when the young man set himself on fire, when he started to run and to release an almost inhuman cry of pain, must people have stopped to stare with dread or confusion at the living torch. When the ambulance took him away, he was still alive. He died in a hospital on Legerova Street three days later.

Palach, an ordinary youngster from Všetaty who lived with his aging mother and studied economics at Prague's Charles University, did not seem predestined to become a hero. He did not stand out at all from other students as a leader or political activist. But he must have been sensitive to the passivity of the majority of his fellow students and citizens in the face of the Soviet occupation. Or perhaps he was not old enough or frightened enough to compromise in the new situation, in the way that the whole of society had done after just a few months. His personal engagement was naive from the start: if only he could have called for action by writing and distributing letters and flyers that made people understand what was happening, surely they would stand up together against the Soviets. But by January 1969, the so-called normalization period had started; the irony is that it was Dubček, the creator of reforms, who was taking the country back on the path to Soviet-style communism—at least until he himself was forced to resign in April 1969. There was no visible opposition. Tens of thousands of Czechs and Slovaks lost their jobs; intellectuals, academics and writers were obliged to take up manual work like taking care of garbage, sweeping streets and washing windows.

The months after August 1968 passed, Palach sank more and

more into despair and he decided to perform an extreme act intended to raise the alarm. In a kind of handwritten testament, a letter to the authorities, he warned that if in five days they did not abolish censorship and ban the newspaper published by the occupying troops, there would be more people burning. It was signed "Torch No. 1." This sent the authorities, the so-called healthy forces that the Soviets had installed parallel to Dubček (who was formally in power until April 1969), into a frenzy. The next "torch," a potential "culprit," must be found. Another self-immolation would mean that they were not in control of the situation. Indeed, a month later, on February 25, a second student, Jan Zajic, burned himself to death in the yard of a house on Wenceslas Square. He did not manage to run into the street, as he had planned to do.

Both Palach and Zajic involuntarily became heroes in this tragedy. Standing at that spot in 1970 and remembering Palach, myself a young mother, I could not help thinking of his mother, Libuše. How do you tell a mother that her son, her boy, has just been taken to hospital because he set himself on fire? Could any mother understand this act? It was enough to think of my child back home to know how hard it must have been for his mother to hear that. There was no way to accept that her son Jan would have done this, taken his life for whatever reason, without even saying goodbye to her. . . .

Palach's story doesn't end with his death. Afterward, the police attempted to frame Jan as a feeble-minded young man who acted in a moment of madness, during which he was not entirely himself. Libuše Palachova and a young lawyer, Dagmar Burešova, dared to fight the powers that be to have Jan's name cleared. When they took to court a party official who was a member of the Central Committee, Vilem Novy, he also declared Jan to be mentally unstable and dismissed his act as that of a lunatic and nothing to do with political protest. To sue a party official in 1969 was unheard of. To search for the truth even more so. Both women must have been hugely audacious and stubbornly brave. As Novy cynically remarks in the HBO Europe series based on this event, *Burning Bush* (2013), directed by Agnieszka Holland, "Truth is what is beneficial for the people." The series captures well the spirit of the time, which was not one of open defiance—or of indifference either—but rather of unwilling compliance. People were told that the way to survive the occupation was to put their heads down and shut up or else . . . the Hungarian scenario would follow. The possible fatalities, the dark memory of the thousands killed in Budapest—it would have taken extraordinary bravery to risk that.

The trial of Novy shows the other, brave and really civilized face of citizens of Czechoslovakia. There was no other country in the Soviet bloc where it would have been possible to bring a senior party official to court, and just after the occupation at that. Elsewhere, in the USSR itself or in Hungary or Poland, any such attempt would have been stopped before it had even begun. However, the spirit of the short-lived Prague Spring of reforms lingered for several months afterward. There is a telling episode in the autobiography of the Czech writer Ivan Klíma when the secret police come to his apartment to conduct a search and his wife demands they take off their shoes! Such civil behavior even on the part of secret police, who obligingly entered the apartment barefoot to rummage through his things, demonstrates the difference between Czechoslovakia and any other communist society. It also illustrates what Dubček had in mind on that fatal morning when he appealed to citizens to continue as usual with their daily lives.

Of course, the secret police tried to stop the Palach case from going to court and intimidated and threatened both the mother and her lawyer, who nevertheless ended up winning the case. Moreover, Burešova lived to see the collapse of communism in 1989 and become the first minister of justice in the new democratic Czechoslovakia. The name of Libuše's son was cleared of slander and his memory preserved. She no longer had her son, but Czechoslovakia had its symbol of 1968.

Standing there, in the shadow of the monumental dark façade in 1970, I recalled how youngsters of Paris and Prague had very different faiths. Paris and Prague, although less than one thousand kilometers away from each other, were worlds apart at that time. Asked by Western journalists just weeks before the occupation about what they thought of Western youths, Czech students responded: "We don't understand those Paris riots. Those students were so destructive, cutting down trees, destroying cars. . . . They don't seem to know how lucky they are."

While rebels in Paris stood up against consumerism as well as bourgeois values and ways of life, in Prague young people desired just that. Moreover, Paris students wanted to put culture at the service of a leftist ideology—while in Prague they wanted to get rid of ideology. That process had not started with the reforms in the spring of 1968, but years earlier, with the works of Ludvik Vaculik, Milan Kundera, Ivan Klíma and Josef Škvorecky, with playwrights like Václav Havel and Pavel Kohout and film directors like Miloš Forman and Jirí Menzel—to name but a few. In the decades after the occupation, however, while Czechoslovak authors were forced to sweep garbage from the streets or to emigrate, French authors of the same generation gained more and more importance and influence in culture and philosophy—the French "new philosophers" being a case in point. The occupation marked Eastern Europe for the next twenty years and created an even greater division in an already politically divided continent.

With the demise of the Prague Spring ended the last attempt of communist reformers in the Soviet bloc to introduce some liberal changes to the totalitarian system. The invasion of Czechoslovakia finished that illusion. It was probably the beginning of the end of communism as well because, after Prague, it became clear that nothing at all was going to be reformed. If anything, the Prague Spring showed that communism is like a wool sweater: pull a thread and the whole thing comes undone. Which is why what happened there was decisive in comparison to whatever else happened during the memorable year of 1968. The crucial political, economic and cultural differences between the two parts of Europe have still not disappeared, not even fifty years afterward. One of the reasons for this is that we in the East are so bad at looking back and learning from history. We realized this only in hindsight; even the last president of the Soviet Union, Mikhail Gorbachev (the last to believe in communism too), naively believed in the late 1980s that he could pull off reforms similar to Dubček's.

The Western powers, however, back then did not even contemplate a change in the Cold War balance of power for such a small, unimportant Central European country. One recalls Neville Chamberlain in 1938, a few days before Hitler annexed part of Czechoslovakia, Sudetenland, declaring, "How horrible, fantastic, incredible it is that we should be digging trenches and trying

on gas-masks here because of a quarrel in a faraway country between people of whom we know nothing." Neither was a change in
the balance of power considered just a few years ago, when Russia
occupied Crimea in Ukraine in 2014.

Even if Jan Palach's death did not succeed in awakening the
consciousness of his compatriots and prompt them to rebel, his act
of self-sacrifice must have hurt; it must have left deep scars on the
social fabric; it must have tinted the country's conscience and the
memory of millions who felt not only helpless, but morally crushed
by Palach's desperate—and, as it seemed at the time, useless—act
of suicide by self-immolation.

His case makes you wonder whether there must have been a
deeper reason for his deciding to act upon his beliefs in such a radical way. Palach certainly did what he did on purpose, in order to
gain as much attention as possible from the authorities who could
not have ignored or covered up such an act of public self-immolation.
On the other hand, it seemed confusing, because it was so dramatic, so heroic, so uncharacteristic for a Czech person. After all,
the image we have from popular culture and literature is of *The
Good Soldier Schwejk*. The title character in Jaroslav Hašek's immensely popular and widely translated satirical novel is a quiet and
unassuming ordinary person who survives troubles not by drawing attention to himself but by keeping calm and keeping his feet
warm. Yet there is another tradition in the same culture, of people
like the medieval religious reformer Jan Hus or the former dissident and then president Václav Havel, who were ready to spend
years in prison or even be burned at the stake for their principles
and beliefs. The seemingly ordinary young student Jan Palach actually acted in a way that followed their line of thought.

On that day, long ago, I felt an acute awareness of history. A human being of my age had set himself on fire. I could not imagine his pain while his skin and flesh were burning, because such pain is unimaginable. What I could identify with is the frustration and anger that led to this pain. Yet no act is useless if it is preserved in both history and memory. If it is not erased on purpose or forgotten. Even so, a scar remains—an unwanted and unintentional symbol of 1968, a cry of someone who did not resign himself to the tanks. Regardless of today's commemorations or the lack of them, my generation of East Europeans and that of my daughter could not forget Palach. Nor could they forget the rupture between the West and the East in Europe that followed 1968.

But what about the younger ones? What do they remember today, whether as descendants of the victims or of the perpetrators? It was a good question to ask on the fiftieth anniversary of an event that influenced the destiny of communism for the worse. Opinion polls conducted ahead of the anniversary revealed some interesting facts. A poll by Czech Public Radio in June 2018 found that among Czechs aged eighteen to sixty-five, one out of four persons could not say what happened in 1968 before the Soviet-led invasion and after the occupation. In the case of those aged eighteen to thirty-four, just over 50 percent knew about 1968. By way of comparison, nearly half of the Russian population says it knows nothing about the invasion at all; more than a third say the Soviet Union was correct to intervene in Czechoslovakia in 1968, according to polling data obtained by *The Guardian* in 2018. Just 10 percent of Russian eighteen- to thirty-five-year-olds said they knew about the Prague Spring.

Perhaps today it is more a question of who wants to remember

'68. For Russians, the lack of knowledge of history is perhaps understandable, not only because they were the occupying force, but also because of the political context—i.e., the 2014 occupation of Crimea, which Russia's government would like to justify. But how about the generation of victims, their children and grandchildren? As in other post-communist countries, they do not know because they do not learn such things at school. Nor do they discuss them at home.

When comrade Dubček spoke on the radio in Prague and told citizens not to resist because resistance to such power is useless, how did he know that? After all, resistance to Adolf Hitler also seemed useless. Maybe the Soviets did not need more bloodshed after Budapest and would therefore withdraw from Prague? Is this the reason that those who did listen to Dubček avoid talking today, President Zeman included? But, as the argument sometimes goes, why would someone born in the last three decades even bother about what happened in 1968 and its legacy? The answer is simple: Because it is history and because history influences us all; it has shaped people in that part of the world for decades. In my experience, there is still a gap between history and memory in the former communist countries—as in this case of the shameful commemoration in Prague of the fiftieth anniversary of the occupation shows. Considering that, fifty years ago, history existed only as "official history" approved by the Communist Party, individual memory worked as a kind of correction to that official history, i.e., it was closer to historical events.

There is one particularly symbolic photo from occupied Bratislava in August 1968. It was taken by the photographer Ladislav Bielik on Safarikovo Square. A small boy stands in short pants with his hands in his pockets in a typical pose of curiosity. He is leaning above a makeshift cross and the flowers marking the spot where one victim was killed, while behind him in white letters someone has written on a housefront "Fallen for freedom." The boy in the photo is named Samuel Abraham. He left Czechoslovakia for Canada and returned after the collapse of communism. He is now the rector of a liberal arts college in Bratislava. In a private letter he remembers the day of his brush with history:

> So, here I am, probably on August 23 or 24, looking at an improvised monument to a female student who was killed there on August 21 at noon. I remember much dark blood on the ground. We had just returned from Yugoslavia and that sweater was green-black.
>
> I lived just fifty meters from Safarikovo Square, where shooting started at exactly noon on August 21. I was on the square then—soldiers had been marching through the city since 9 a.m. I escaped our apartment—my mother was quite afraid when I returned. The marching soldiers reached the square around 11:30 a.m. and there was some confrontation—we were throwing wooden sticks (I remember there were black-and-white striped sticks—strange that I can remember the pattern) and then the shooting started. I was in the middle of the square and started to run in the opposite direction from the Comenius University building at which the machine gun aimed—first going upward and then downward. I see still that movement of the firing gun, before I ran for cover, killing two people on the square. The shooting was coordinated—in other parts of Bratislava as well—altogether eight people were

killed, . . . Being eight at the time, I remember vividly the
events and the atmosphere, more so than any other period of
my life.

And then Abraham turns from his experience of a moment in history that formed his life to the big history that affected everyone in Czechoslovakia.

The self-immolation of Jan Palach was not a protest against
the Russians but an act begging fellow Czech and Slovak
citizens to stick together and continue to resist peacefully and
stick to the reforms. There was supposed to be a self-immolation
every week by other young people from the group. . . . His tragic
death—at once a sacrifice made for us and us being
reprimanded for giving in—was the greatest reminder of our
humiliation and servitude throughout the so-called
normalization period led by Brezhnev's puppet from 1969 to
1989, our own Slovak Gustav Husak. The worst part was that
we thought we would not live to see the end of all this. That was
a daily debate at our house. In order to avoid sad talk about
politics, there was talk about art, books, philosophy; and I
remember lots of singing, often accompanied by alcohol and the
artists and intellectuals who came to our big apartment just
fifty meters from the square. I could not stand the double life
shaped by the official propaganda at school and media, and the
graveness, human sadness witnessed at home or in any private
debate. So I emigrated via Yugoslavia, as Tito was dying in
August 1980.

Time and again we see that history, "official history," and individual memory do not necessarily overlap. Just as Samuel Abraham will not forget that August day, people should not forget this photo of a boy trying to comprehend what he had witnessed.

Women, Harassment, East, West

Are some women more resistant to violence?

Imagine a couple, a man and a woman, sitting in a restaurant somewhere in Stockholm. It is Saturday evening, they have just had a nice dinner and after the question "Your place or mine?" they decide to go to his place. In the apartment, they have a glass of wine and start kissing on a couch. But because they met only recently, they wonder how best to proceed. Usually people do not need instructions on how to get into bed and make love. But after #MeToo, the atmosphere changed.

A new law came into force in Sweden as of July 1, 2018, that requires the explicit consent of both partners; otherwise, intercourse is considered rape, even if no violence is involved. An agreement in words or the clear demonstration of a willingness to have sex is needed. You can kiss and fondle and that should be enough; the body language on both sides sends clear signals. But recently, in many cases ten or twenty years after the event, women have claimed that it was not consensual sex that they had. The man kissing on the couch might remember exactly what happened. But in the case of a subsequent complication, how would he prove that sex was consensual? A serious couple—quite usual in the case of Swedes—rightly debates whether to sign a document, record their statements or take some extra step in order for their consent to be proven in law. In the meantime, the moment passes and what looked like a promise ends with a kiss on the cheek.

The situation described is of course a caricature, as consent is always necessary and it is usually the case that when people go to bed, it is because they both want to. Except when one, usually a woman, does not want to, in which case it is good that there is a law that she can fall back upon.

Nevertheless, it is not pleasant when the state enters your bedroom, even when it is at its most benevolent, even when it wants to protect you. It is scary that the state should protect you, that it defines what is good for you even when it comes to intimacy. For those of us who remember Nicolae Ceausescu's dictatorship in Romania, when women were subjected to monthly visits to a gynecologist for a pregnancy test, any attempt of the state to open a door into a bedroom sounds a bit . . . well, too much. As does, for example, the pressure of the Catholic Church on a state to completely ban abortion like in Poland. Unfair comparisons? No, because they deal with the same thing: women, bodies and intimacy.

And yet if the latest feminist campaign does not play a role in legislative change, then it will still not be successful.

The #MeToo campaign against sexual harassment and violence is perhaps one of the most important things to have happened lately to both women and feminism. #MeToo started in the United States in October 2017 as a hashtag on social media that went viral, swept Europe and created a new social situation in terms of changing the perception of what is socially acceptable in men's behavior toward (mostly) women. The movement created an acute awareness of the fact that most women do indeed experience sexual harassment, assault and violence. When only a few of them speak up, they go unnoticed by the media and society in general. But when thousands speak, everybody listens. #MeToo empowered women to speak up not only for themselves, but also because it matters to other women too and because together they could make a change.

It seems that the campaign offered a much-needed focus, a single issue of which most women had some experience and with which they could identify, something that had been lacking in the feminist movement ever since the struggle for equal rights decades ago. This new focus could be interpreted as a consequence of a range of issues, from the fragmentation caused by "gender identity" politics and gender fluidity to the struggle for inclusive language, all the way to inclusive bathrooms. Of course, feminism is needed in every single aspect of life, but sometimes it needs a single, clearly defined aim in order to achieve social and legal changes. In this instance, it was the campaign to stop sexual assault.

When it comes to legal matters, #MeToo is not without blemishes. On the contrary, it was confusing to see that mass allegations were not followed up with anything like an equal number of legal proceedings. Many men resigned under pressure, without having the chance to defend themselves in a court of law. Many paid with their careers because a claim of harassment was not differentiated from that of sexual assault or rape, as if there are no degrees of hell. This is because to begin with, in the midst of the avalanche of denunciations, the use of violence was not established as a key factor when it came to the perpetrator's liability. Someone touching your leg under the table or groping you is in no way the same as the use of violence to rape you. This is why, according to *The Economist*, just one year after the #MeToo explosion, public opinion seemed to be increasingly supportive of opinions such as "men who sexually harassed women at work twenty years ago should keep their jobs" (up from 28 to 36 percent) or "women who complain about harassment cause more problems than they solve" (up from 29 to 31 percent). Or that false accusations constitute a bigger problem than attacks that go unreported or unpunished (up from 13 to 18 percent). Even if the increase is small, it indicates a distinct change in the popular mood.

But objections to harassment were not equally distributed in all social strata, even in the United States. Not all women felt that they had to speak out against it, especially those who could scarcely count upon the support of the public or of powerful women. Ordinary women were much more reluctant to risk revealing their bosses to be sexual predators. It became clear that if #MeToo is to change from a campaign into a movement, it has to encompass all strata of society and not stop at the top.

The campaign in the United States is different than that in Europe. Some parts of Europe have remained almost untouched by it. Indeed, when traveling from north to south, and from west to east, it becomes apparent that women's voices are heard less and less. When we reach the Balkans, they turn into a mere whisper. As if no harassment ever happened there. These campaigns will always have a local color—in France, men were called "pigs," which is not the case in, say, Germany. By the way, in France a prominent actress, Catherine Deneuve, and a group of one hundred public figures denounced the #MeToo campaign, defending men's "freedom to pester" women. However, the attitude is rapidly changing even there.

One wonders about the countries where the campaign has barely registered. In Romania, for example, the effects are negligible compared with the tectonic shift in Sweden, where the new law on consent was promptly passed in parliament and one man wound up in jail for two years for a rape committed in 2011. This was a major scandal, because the man, Jean-Claude Arnault, is the husband of a member of the Swedish Academy. With its reputation tarnished by the case, the Academy decided not to award a Nobel Prize in Literature in 2018 and instead to award two prizes a year later. Meanwhile, in the United Kingdom the defense secretary, Michael Fallon, had to quit because of his harassment of a number of women.

If we imagine the situation that took place in a room in Stockholm but now taking place in a room in Sofia, Bulgaria, then we can be certain that there will be no deliberation about documenting consent. But what if a woman changes her mind and a man then uses force? Here is the difference: not many people would ever know and nothing much would happen. The police and the courts rarely deal with rape if at all, except in drastic cases where there are severe physical consequences.

Let us not go as far as bed. Let us stay with harassment, as the whole movement started with revealing unwanted touches of varying degrees, ranging from rather unpleasant to violent. What is considered harassment in Bulgaria? And is this experienced in the same way in Stockholm as it is in Sofia?

No, it is not. But even among Western countries, understandings of what constitutes sexual harassment vary greatly. A YouGov poll from 2017 in Germany, Britain, France, Denmark, Sweden, Finland and Norway revealed that, when it comes to sexual jokes, German women are more tolerant than British, while Danish women barely react. Only 37 percent of British women object when a man puts his arm around a woman's waist, compared with 72 percent of French women taking offense; even a man looking at their breasts upsets half of them.

The differences between countries about what is perceived as sexual harassment were demonstrated years before #MeToo, in a major 2014 study by the European Union Agency for Fundamental Rights involving 42,000 women from all twenty-eight EU member states. The results are striking. In Scandinavian countries, 81 percent of women had been harassed, while in Poland and Romania the figure was 32 percent. Bulgaria ranked lowest, with 24 percent. Overall, however, only 6 percent of women had reported serious sexual harassment to colleagues, and only 4 percent had contacted the police; less than 1 percent had spoken to a lawyer. Again, the figures were highest in Denmark, Sweden and France. When mapping what is considered harassment, the dividing line between east and west is striking.

If there are such differences in perception of harassment between Western countries, then what about the way in which reactions to #MeToo vary between Western countries and former communist countries?

In Hungary, it has had some impact, albeit largely limited to the cultural sphere and liberal circles. In Poland, nearly 35,000 posts with the tags #MeToo and #JaTeż, including those by celebrities, appeared in social media between October 15 and 22, 2017. In subsequent months, however, the campaign lost momentum—perhaps not surprising given that, according to a report by Eurobarometer (European Commission public opinion surveyer) on gender-based violence, as many as 30 percent of Poles think that sex without the consent of the other person might be justified, depending on the circumstances (the figure averages 27 percent across Europe as a whole). In the Czech Republic, public radio reported that every tenth woman in the country has been raped, but only about 10 percent of them ever report the crime to the police, while just 2 percent of perpetrators are ever convicted in court. In response to the #MeToo campaign, the European commissioner for gender equality, the Czech politician Věra Jourová, revealed that she too had been a victim of sexual violence and called on women to join the movement.

Although Romania has one of the highest rates of violence against women in Europe, police figures reveal that only thirty-four cases of various kinds of sexual assault and rape were filed in 2017. But hundreds of stories were shared on social media. Among them, a member of parliament, Florina Presada, revealed that she herself had been harassed. However, the campaign petered out before bearing any further fruit. The same happened in Slovakia. The few stories about sexual harassment that did appear there concerned men who were deceased.

"In Slovakia, we often react in a bizarre way when a woman reveals she has been abused or experienced sexual harassment," said Ľubica Rozborová of the Department of Gender Equality and Equal Opportunities in the Ministry of Labor. "We tend to distrust her, question her words or blame her for having caused the incident." At least there has been some reaction in these countries; in Estonia or Croatia, for example, there has been next to nothing:

all that appeared in the latter were a few sensationalist articles in the media, to the dismay of Croatian feminists.

It seems obvious that the #MeToo campaign in Eastern Europe cannot be compared with that in the West, in terms either of intensity and duration or of actual consequences, be it demoting men in powerful positions or widespread public support. Of course, the question is why women in Eastern Europe, who are probably harassed as much as, if not more than, women in the West, do not perceive such behavior as harassment. Are they more tolerant? Are they brought up differently? Or is their perception of what is and what is not permitted variously influenced by the region's different political regimes?

I would say that most likely, women experience harassment, but they do not talk about it, because they are aware that they cannot do anything about it. Describing how she was sexually harassed as a child and then as an adolescent in Romania, Maria Bucur writes in *Public Seminar* journal: "I never felt free to discuss my fear of being sexually assaulted, because there was no precedent, no language, no acknowledgement of its pervasiveness."

When I was a young girl, but old enough to be harassed verbally while walking down the street or physically on public transport, it did not occur to me to tell my mother, a teacher or anyone about it. It was too embarrassing, and in addition I lacked both the words and the courage, because society simply did not perceive such behavior in men to be offensive. How many times in a bus or tram have women felt a man pressing up against their bottom, a hand reaching for a leg or brushing against their breasts? Too many to even count, because it belonged to the customary behavior of men there, like smoking, drinking and cursing. I was aware that I should not provoke men, that I should try to move away in such a situation. However, this was quite impossible when I got stuck on a packed bus or in a queue. I also noticed smiles of approval by other men, as if shouting obscenities were a rude but still acceptable kind of complimenting a woman. It was senseless to report a man for his habitual behavior; and to whom would one report him? It seemed extreme to go to the police, who, in a communist country, were considered to be an instrument of power to be used against the people, not to help them. I knew that the blame would inevitably fall on me anyway—either for the way I dressed or my behavior. Women everywhere know these "arguments" by heart, and perhaps in some countries and cultures they are more pronounced than in others. Most of us would feel guilty for no reason, and there was simply nobody to cry out to.

This is also reflected in the #MeToo campaign nowadays: women know that they would be blamed for what is still considered "much ado about nothing."

Later in life, the harassment continued, at work or while studying. It was expressed in other ways as well: besides unwanted kisses and hugs, there was groping too; explicit suggestions and indecent proposals were added to the list. However, we were grown up and better able to fend off unwanted contact. In a very patriarchal culture, girls grew up experiencing harassment as unpleasant but more or less ordinary behavior. It seems to me that, indeed, the pervasiveness of sexual harassment was acknowledged and that this was itself the very reason that such things were tolerated in society.

I remember one telling episode that took place in 1978. It was on the occasion of Drug-ca Žena, the first international conference on women in Belgrade. Several well-known feminists attended, like the Italian writer Dacia Maraini and the German journalist Alice

Schwarzer, along with other participants from abroad. During a sightseeing excursion one day, they were shocked by men's behavior in the streets, the shouting of comments and the gestures. Although they did not understand the language, they got the meaning. The colleagues from Belgrade who accompanied them were too ashamed to translate the men's words literally and tried to downplay the whole episode. The guests were clearly surprised at both sets of behavior, those of the men themselves and of the local feminists who tried to brush it aside. However, at that time we—the ex-Yugoslav feminists—did not know better. We had not yet heard that this is what is called sexual harassment.

Forty years later, the lack of response to #MeToo in Eastern Europe is due to not only the social stigma, but to the fear of exposing oneself to ridicule, hostility and possible consequences at work—which women everywhere experience. On top of all of this, there is no tradition of voicing one's problems. Perhaps it is hard to understand that society has to create an environment in which one would recognize such behavior as harassment and feel that she or he could report it. In the West women have less problem doing so, although the majority of domestic violence and rape still remains unreported even there. In Sweden it has been normal to report harassment for many decades now without feeling any embarrassment, whereas this happened only more recently in the United States with #MeToo.

However, in Eastern Europe the past still has a strong hold on the present. There is a mentality that comes of the condition of formal emancipation on the one hand and a very patriarchal society on the other.

When considering the reactions of women in Eastern Europe to this campaign against sexual harassment, abuse and violence, an important issue is largely overlooked: that of domestic violence. It could well be that the "domesticated" everyday violence witnessed and experienced in most of these societies accounts for the lack of response to #MeToo. Of course, the situation varies from country to country, but we all grew up more or less familiar with an occasional slap even in the best of families and corporal punishment for children ("If you beat them with a rod, they will not die!" was a popular attitude), whether at home or at school. Though it did not happen often, it was no scandal if a teacher slapped a pupil at the primary school I attended. Not because of communism as such, but because it so happened that the communist regime was introduced or imposed in underdeveloped, mostly agricultural countries with strong patriarchal societies. The more patriarchal the society, the more violence one experienced or witnessed, domestic and elsewhere. Yet hard numbers on domestic violence were conspicuously absent from the statistics the state produced for every field of human life, and we were left with very rough estimates and intuitive insights, with stories instead of facts and numbers.

To say that women in the former communist countries were used to violence and therefore did not consider sexual harassment a big thing would be to go too far. But the fact that violence in the family was rarely reported or the subject of a trial in a court of law certainly indicates that it was not seen as a big problem, either within the family or within society at large. If anything, it was perceived as part and parcel of alcoholism, a serious problem at the time. Again, a survey from 2012 by the EU Agency for Fundamental Rights gives us some idea of what we are talking about when we say violence. The countries with the highest percentage of physical, sexual, etc., violence committed by a partner or a non-partner and experienced by victims above the age of fifteen are Denmark, at 52 percent; Finland, 47 percent; and Sweden, 46 percent. At the other end of the spectrum are once again Eastern European countries such as Poland, at 19 percent, and Croatia, 21 percent. A few years later, in 2016 in Croatia, 78 percent of persons murdered in domestic violence were women. In ten recent years some 250 women have been killed, 15,000 per year were registered as maltreated and one in ten experience domestic violence.

It is hard to believe that Nordic women—according to these statistics at least—suffer more violence from the hands of men than Polish and Croatian women do. Other parameters in these countries would lead one to draw very different conclusions. The difference must rest with the definition of violence—something that is shaped by society. Obviously, in a strongly patriarchal society, women are conditioned to stand more violence. This, then, combines with the victim-blaming attitude of society, which continues to be more common in Eastern Europe even today.

That this was and remains the reality, regardless of the general level of women's emancipation, is one of the paradoxes of life under communism, as well as under post-communism.

On the one hand, women's rights were built into the communist state and its legal system, guaranteeing women all the basic rights—from voting to property ownership, from education to divorce, from equal pay for equal work to the right to have control over their own bodies. In the region of the former Yugoslavia just 150 years ago or so, almost 90 percent of women could not read or write. Women weren't even able to sign their names. They could not inherit property, divorce or choose whether to have a baby. They received the right to study only about 110 years ago. The former Croatian female president Kolinda Grabar-Kitarović is a good example when it comes to changes brought about by communism in a very short time. From her disenfranchised grandma to the woman who grew up in a society where there were equal rights and became president: this certainly demonstrates what communism did for women by emancipating them "from above."

The change, however, did not happen without women actively participating, whether in combat during World War II or, after it, organizing women and teaching them to write properly in the Antifascist Front of Women (AFZ). But although this was an independent organization, it was soon taken over by the Communist Party and made into the *communist* women's organization, an instrument of party power that was concerned less with women and their needs than with spreading communist ideology.

In such circumstances, feminism was considered to be a "suspicious activity." Since women were emancipated, there was no need to discuss women's rights, so the official argument went. It was as if women lived in an ideal world but were not fully aware of it, or failed to appreciate the fact. And those who tried to enlighten women about the real situation became suspicious elements. Women who attempted to mention the word "feminism" or try to publicly discuss it in the 1980s were accused by the authorities of "importing foreign, bourgeois ideas." Prejudices against Western, and especially American, feminists were disseminated by the press; not only were these women said to be man haters who were too ugly to find a husband, they were also burning bras! Probably this bra-burning "argument" against feminists was most effective in precisely that part of the world where it was hard to buy a good bra. Feminists there were considered to be a kind of dissident at best— but they were more likely to be seen as traitors.

However, domestic violence was therefore a good starting point for the first informal feminist groups and writings, like the group Žena i društvo in Zagreb, Yugoslavia, in the early eighties—the very first in that part of Europe. Feminists from that group tried to explain in the media that violence is not a normal part of women's lives and that they should not put up with it—rather, they should report it to the police and sometimes file for divorce. And although a divorce was possible, it was nevertheless a difficult decision because of the lack of apartments. Renting an apartment was expensive, almost prohibitively so, and there were very few apartments to rent. You could go back to your parents. Or stay in the same apartment, divorced. So the couple's finances often led to a decision not to divorce.

It took a lot of time and persuasion to establish the first emergency hotline and shelter for battered women in Zagreb. And when the law changed so that police could intervene in domestic quarrels in order to prevent violence, it was considered a great victory. Except that police intervened very rarely. In the confrontation between the law and tradition, tradition was winning.

In daily life, women experienced an obvious gap between proclaimed principles, laws and institutions on the one hand and reality, which was ruled by patriarchal customs, on the other. This "emancipation from above," even with the initial involvement of women, functioned differently than "emancipation from below"—the grassroots movements that emerged with the struggle of women in the West during the past hundred years. Thus emancipation from above left generations of women with no knowledge of how to demand their rights, believing perhaps that someone else would take up and fight for their cause on their behalf.

Even now, three decades after the collapse of communism, women in Eastern Europe still are reluctant to voice their concerns—about sexual harassment, among other topics. But is this lumping together of women under the common denominator of the "communist past" even legitimate, since Eastern Europeans no longer belong to a single block? I think it is, because that very denominator still glues them together and, in many ways, influences their way of life.

After the collapse of communism, most countries in that part of Europe experienced a renaissance of nationalism and of religion— precisely the two things that were most suppressed under communism. And patriarchal culture never disappeared. This is partly reflected in the post-1989 pro-choice controversy. The right to choose whether or not to give birth is a cornerstone of women's emancipation, and efforts to deny or restrict this right point to a lot of other problems in the political, social, economic and legal position of women in every society.

At the end of 2014, the media reported that more and more gynecologists in public hospitals in Croatia were refusing to perform abortions—in a country where abortion has been legal since 1969. It is not enough that, for the majority of women, terminating a pregnancy is an agonizing decision. Nor is it enough that, unless you can pay extra, it is a painful procedure. In Croatia, you will be turned away from one hospital only to discover that in another doctors do not perform the procedure either, although they are obliged by law to do so. Since 1996, doctors, nurses and pharmacists have been able to refuse any involvement in abortions on the grounds of conscientious objection. The aim, of course, is to discourage women from having an abortion.

Women's voices have been absent (except in Poland) in a debate that is of vital importance to them. Young women, those who should be the most concerned, simply did not react. There were no mass protests, as one might have expected, either on city squares or in social media. At first sight it seems strange that the new generation of women, growing up in a democratic system, does not respond to what can only be described as a blatant infringement of their rights—and their health as well. But here we are again, back to square one, to the same old arguments that apply all too often to harassment or domestic violence, to the toned-down perception of the problem and the lack of experience of confronting and dealing with it, a condition that is perpetuated by women habitually acting on their own. The idea that women should support other women to achieve common objectives does not exist in Eastern Europe and never did. Moreover, women participating in governments there seem not to recognize gender problems are a political issue. Left to their own devices, women are not doing as much as they could. It's as if the most important lesson—that socioeconomic downturns can cause a backlash and the revocation of the basic right to choose—has yet to be learned.

But the example of Poland is quite different and gives others hope too. In 1993 abortion was banned except in cases of the malformation of the fetus, of rape or of the mother's life being endangered. At that point there was no mass public reaction to the proposed ban. Women were mostly trying to survive the hard times of transition. They felt too powerless to stand up for their rights. However, as of 2009, a powerful organization called Women's Congress (Kongres Kobiet) appeared. It proved capable of mobilizing huge numbers of women. In October 2016, after one hundred thousand women took to the streets to protest proposals for a total ban on abortion, the government had to backtrack.

In other countries, with the political focus on economic transformation and the building of democratic structures, women's rights were not a top priority, not even to themselves.

The situation of women in societies caught up in post-1989 transition is not easy. But women have had a hard time in the West as well, where they also suffer from underemployment, pay inequality, the glass ceiling, loss of status. Women engage less than men in politics in the West too. All this has gotten worse over the past decade. The financial crisis was indeed a common denominator. It hit all of Europe—East and West, men and women. The most worrying consequence of the financial crisis for women, however, has been the rapid dismantling of the welfare state and the pauperization of women. Fewer women are working, despite the fact that more of them have better qualifications. In the EU, women's employment is increasing (66.6 percent in 2017, compared with 78.1 percent for men), but there are still fewer women employed than men; those who are employed generally have less well-paid jobs than men. The gender pay gap, which averages 16 percent in the EU, persists even though women do better at school and university than men. This means that women get smaller pensions and are poorer in old age.

Differences in reactions to the #MeToo campaign stem from different histories and divergences in the lives of women. Totalitarian political regimes are part of that phenomena because they rendered women speechless, made them silent. The lives of women are even more tough now than before, at least in terms of preserving rights and privileges, employment prospects and equal pay for the same job. Many cannot afford to have a child. Many migrate to the West in search of a better life. In such conditions of existential insecurity, the issue of sexual harassment, pressing as it is, is just not a priority for women to put up a fight about.

The right to speak out against sexual harassment, assault and violence is an important one. Yet the struggle to exercise that right should be seen for what it is, as the latest episode in a long, difficult and sometimes painful struggle of women for power over their own bodies. In Eastern Europe, however, the fact that this right did not have the same impact as in the West means that the gap that opened up in the past has not closed as quickly as we believed it would.

Many leading women in culture, business leaders, politicians and entertainment, especially in the United States, have hurried to proclaim the #MeToo campaign a revolutionary movement. But to become that, it would have to be much wider and broader in scope so as to reach everywhere—and receive the same substantial support everywhere too.

Fueling Fear

*Why nationalism
demands a response*

Octover 2017. Barcelona, Spain. Catalan pro-independence protests: hundreds of thousands rally in the streets, carrying Catalan flags and banners with the slogan "Catalonia Is Not Spain" and chanting "*Llibertat!*" At some points, there were as many as 450,000 pro-independence protesters in the streets.

November 11, 2017. Independence Day in Warsaw, Poland. The police estimated that 60,000 people marched in the largely young crowd. Many chanted "Fatherland"; their banners read "White Europe," "Europe Will Be White" and "Clean Blood." *The Wall Street Journal* reported that some of the marchers had flown in from Hungary, Slovakia and Spain and waved flags and symbols that those countries used during their wartime collaboration with Nazi Germany. Polish state television called the procession a "great march of patriots."

These two recent episodes, one illustrating separatism, the other racism, are symbolic of the new forces that have been emerging in the EU over the last couple of years, forces that thrive on fear and call for new walls to be erected, for pure blood, for the exclusion of Others and for division.

Nationalism is an ideology that needs an enemy; it constitutes itself in confrontation with the Other—whoever that might be at the moment. As George Orwell wrote in "Notes on Nationalism" in 1945: "Patriotism is of its nature defensive, both militarily and culturally. Nationalism, on the other hand, is inseparable from the desire for power. The abiding purpose of every nationalist is to secure more power and more prestige, not for himself but for the nation or other unit in which he has chosen to sink his own individuality."

Patriotism does not demand comparison and conflict. And because it is a private feeling—in the domain of memory, childhood, landscape, food—no justification is needed.

The fact that nationalism, by contrast, needs confrontation, and is therefore dangerous, is often neglected.

Not so long ago, at the beginning of the nineties, while the rest of Europe was uniting or hoping to unite by joining the EU, one country was falling apart in bloody wars. That country was Yugoslavia—the best-off communist country there had been, and the one least expected to descend into secessionism, separatism, ethnic cleansing, civil war or aggression. The reason it did was nationalism.

Today it is more important than ever to understand how nationalism came to play such a decisive role, to the point of a breakup, because it looks as if Yugoslavia managed to export it to the EU, a community built precisely to avoid nationalism and war. A paradox? Yes, to the extent that it was not expected. But now it seems to be the logical consequence of events set in motion after the collapse of communism in 1989. It is as if there were suddenly a need for self-legitimization and self-confirmation, a need to again articulate who you are through language, as in the Baltic countries, which have a large Russian minority. Or to rewrite history, as in Croatia, in opposition to the "official history" interpreted by the Communist Party.

The quick accession of former Soviet bloc countries to the EU was meant to overcome differences in history, experience, the economy and culture between Eastern and Western Europe, not taking into account that there is no such thing as a shortcut to the development of democracy. The psychological shock that millions of citizens must have experienced during the collapse of an all-encompassing political system, as well as during the subsequent transition, was barely taken into consideration. East Europeans were supposed to rejoice; they did, but it was short-lived. A decade passed and they accused the EU of neocolonialism, exploitation, creating economic injustice; they complained about the lack of jobs and the democratic deficit.

However, under the communist state's pressure to comply and conform, nationalism proved to be a vital and positive force, keeping alive national identity, culture, language and religion. Therefore, when many started to perceive globalization as a new threat, even a new kind of totalitarianism, especially in Eastern Europe, but also increasingly in the West—the same "identity-protection mechanism" was activated again, reverting to what was familiar.

Frustrations are mounting. Obviously the way to express them is in the rise of radical right parties and separatist movements. But what energizes them now? What provoked slogans like "Clean Blood" and the growing acceptance of extreme nationalism and xenophobia among young people in Hungary, Slovakia and the Czech Republic? Or in Poland, among Europe's most prosperous countries, the only member of the EU that, for example, didn't experience a recession after the financial crisis. Although it had few economic problems, and even fewer immigrants, the government-controlled Polish media broadcast near nightly reports on crimes committed by Muslims in Europe.

Polish historian and former dissident Adam Michnik once said that nationalism is like a virus: it is dormant in every organism and every society but can wake up when the conditions are right. He was speaking about the wars in the former Yugoslavia. But what could be interpreted as the "right conditions" now?

Apparently, the powers that be have—again—underestimated the power of emotion.

It has become obvious that at the root of nationalist passions is fear that immigrants could change our way of life. If nationalist propaganda manages to create fear in people, then the main step toward conflict is taken, the main obstacle overcome. A feeling of insecurity creates fear of the Other, a closing down, a fencing off of Others and, finally, aggression. Even if nationalism in Yugoslavia thirty years ago did not have the same historical roots as contemporary nationalism in, say, Spain or Italy today, it is scary to see the pattern being repeated. Because the psychological mechanism of using fear to evoke hatred works in the very same way—by employing words.

When speaking about the psychological preconditions for the violence and conflicts that nationalism could provoke, the absolute precondition is violence in words, in language itself. If nationalism needs an enemy, it has to be clear who that enemy is. In fact, nationalism has the power to create the enemy by first naming it. Therefore, through the media the nationalist propaganda machine launches the language of division, suspicion and, eventually, hatred. If there was a history of problems between the two sides (as in Catalonia, the Basque country, Belgium or eastern Ukraine), so much the better, because it could then be used—manipulated to divide people and whip up emotions. For that you need strong language. Every conflict is prepared with the use of dangerous words. We can already hear the same words and vocabulary that were last used decades ago.

Interestingly, it seems that problems perceived as real—such as the economic crisis; the loss of faith in compromised politics and politicians, as well as in the Brussels bureaucracy and European unity; and the collapse in the social-democratic welfare system and solidarity principle—were less important as a prompt for unleashing the forces of nationalism. The immediate trigger for mass discontent became the influx of immigrants, or rather the political manipulation connected to this. There are many examples of this, among them Marine Le Pen's cry "Give Us France Back" or the German AfD (Alternative for Germany) party's poster "Stop Islamization."

It is fear of immigrants that connects, say, the separatists of Spain and the Polish right-wing youth, the German AfD and France's Le Pen, Hungary's Viktor Orbán and Geert Wilders in the Netherlands, the True Finns and the Sweden Democrats. The social atmosphere this fear cultivates makes possible the articulation of radical demands and the explosion of nativist political movements all over the EU.

While Catalans are seizing on a moment of general discontent and anxiety, and the influx of immigrants does not seem to be playing a key role in that conflict, it is the response to the presence of immigrants more widely that has enabled a change in the European atmosphere from connivance to separatism. The fact that, for example, Finland took in just a small number of immigrants while Sweden accepted some 163,000 asylum seekers—the most in the EU, in relative terms—but both are experiencing a resurgence in nationalism, shows that, regardless of the real numbers, people are reacting with emotions. In the parlance of the right wingers, all immigrants are Muslims and therefore potential terrorists. This kind of language, which reduces nations to a religion (and the religion of the enemy therefore becomes a threat in itself) is a political use of identity: it was exactly the kind of language that laid the ground for the nationalist wars in the former Yugoslavia. Yet no lesson was learned from that. Not even enough to recognize the signs and dangers of nationalism, so as to respond promptly.

In the same way, today's refugees are no longer allowed to be individuals, not even members of a state or a nation. They are reduced to a religious identity, regardless of whether they themselves are religious or not.

But what are the differences, if any, between the Catalan separatists and Italy's Northern League on the one side, and right-wing movements and parties in Poland, Hungary, the Netherlands, Finland and Germany on the other? Regardless of the historical differences, one can say that they are different in the degree of their desire for separation. Some seem to be halfway out of the Union, others want to depart, while still others want to keep immigrants out and their nation-state ethnically clean. The point is that the politics of exclusion is becoming mainstream, and nationalism and nativism are on the rise.

Europeanism, an identity in the making, has acquired a new meaning: building inner and outer, physical and psychological walls against immigrants.

It is a self-fulfilling prophecy: the fear of immigrants threatens to destroy the very social and political fabric, culture, tradition, religion and way of life that Europeans want to protect. And thus, as Ivan Krastev writes in his book *After Europe*, immigrants may become the ones who determine the destiny of the EU.

The Republic of
North Macedonia

How to construct a better past

I opened my mailbox and found a letter. The pristine white envelope was marked with a stamp from Macedonia—or rather, the Former Yugoslav Republic of Macedonia.

What a strange and cumbersome name, I thought as I held the letter, but I remembered that for almost three decades, since the collapse of the former Yugoslavia, this former republic and then state had lived with an official name that it did not want. Another state, namely Greece, prevented the state from using its preferred name: Macedonia. At the heart of this dispute was ancient history and ancient peoples.

Conflicts between ancient Macedonians and ancient Greeks, the Hellenes, go back over two millennia to the fourth century BCE, when Macedonians conquered the Greek city-states. The Kingdom of Macedonia was then ruled by Philip II, but when he was assassinated in 336 BCE, his son, Alexander, acceded to the throne. Alexander defeated the Persians once and for all and conquered

territories that extended all the way to India and North Africa—
the greatest series of conquests ever.

Today, Greeks, who consider themselves the heirs of ancient
Greeks or Hellenes and of Alexander the Great, strongly oppose
the neighboring state using the name Macedonia, as well as that
nation's flag bearing a version of the Vergina Sun, the royal symbol of the Argead dynasty of Philip II, Alexander's father.

Today's Macedonians feel that Alexander the Great is the "father
of the nation," as it were. However, there is a problem with Alexander as a national idol. Alexander was not of pure Macedonian
blood—his mother, Olympia, was from Epirus—nor did he consider himself Macedonian. He embraced Hellenistic culture and the
teachings of his tutor, Aristotle. As a result of Alexander's conquests, he spread Hellenism all over the known world and made
ancient Greek the lingua franca. Because of that, if Philip II had
lived, he likely would have considered his son a traitor. It seems a
paradox that today's Macedonian nationalists call upon Alexander
in this way; they have obviously decided to ignore the truth in the
name of the "higher aim" of creating a more glorious past.

Who was writing to me from the Former Yugoslav Republic of
Macedonia? I took a single sheet of paper, on which an elderly person had written elegant script with a fountain pen, out of the envelope. I hadn't heard from Biljana for ages, ever since her half
brother—my cousin—had passed away. No one else I know has
such fine handwriting: *Dear Slavenka, it is now a long time since we
last met. Both of us were small girls, you a few years older than me.* . . .

In the early 1960s, my Croatian aunt met a man from the Socialist Republic of Macedonia and married him. Back then, Macedonia
was one of the Yugoslav federal state's six republics, and we be-

lieved that Uncle Tošo was "Macedonian." What else could people living there be but Macedonians? Like Croats living in Croatia or Serbs living in Serbia. But at that time national identity politics were a threat to the unity of Yugoslavia. The two of them spoke Serbo-Croatian to each other, which Tošo knew from school because it was the official language, but my aunt soon learned Macedonian (an officially recognized language in Yugoslavia but not in Bulgaria or Greece, although these countries have a Macedonian minority) and their son grew up speaking both. Uncle Tošo had a daughter from his previous marriage, Biljana, the woman who had written this letter to me. There were some inheritance documents to be sorted out and so after almost an entire lifetime, the letter came.

I met their whole family only once, when they visited us in Rijeka. Back then, Biljana was about six years old, small and plump with lively eyes. We could hardly exchange a word, but we lay together on the beach anyway. We saw little of each other after that because the road from Rijeka in the west of the country is long and it was expensive to travel all the way east of Yugoslavia to Bitola. The bus ride took two days. But also, although part of the same state of Yugoslavia, Macedonia was not only geographically distant but culturally and mentally far removed from Croatia. No wonder, because for centuries they belonged to two different empires. Croatia had been part of the Austro-Hungarian Empire and the territory of Macedonia had been part of the Ottoman Empire, and even though we lived together in the same nation-state for almost fifty years, many of our differences did not disappear, and some 800 kilometers to the southeast was another world that was as exotic to us as Turkey.

Biljana included her daughter Ana's telephone number in her letter. I contacted Ana and decided to travel to Skopje, interested in exploring the Macedonian capital, in addition to attending to these pressing family matters.

FYROM, or the Former Yugoslav Republic of Macedonia, is rarely in the news, but Skopje had recently raised its profile with a project to build a new, better past. In the previous decade, from 2006 to 2016, the government had decided to reinforce the idea of an ancient Macedonian identity by building a series of sculptures, squares and buildings in the manner of the ancient Greeks. Under the nationalist party VMRO-DPNE, the project was officially named Skopje 2014. The idea of sharing the same ethnicity as Alexander (even if he was not pure Macedonian) must have been such an appealing notion to many in this country that it was worth every penny of the alleged 600 million euros spent in part on various efforts to revive or invent history. The remainder was, independent sources claim, embezzled. Creating a nation from scraps of ancient history, myths and legends is a big political, economic and cultural undertaking. It is probably also the last such project in Europe today. Clearly, the battle for the right to use Macedonia in the name of the state was the first step in this process; but later on, sculptures and architecture also have a role to play. Symbols are important when feverishly creating a national identity in such a short time. When building the nation on territory where political efforts to make the state lack any continuity, there is no choice but to reinterpret, re-create and even invent the past.

On the other hand, the idea, or rather the accusation, of the neighboring state that these people are stealing the Greeks' cultural inheritance, symbols and names—and therefore appropriating the identity of the rightful owners—is also highly problematic. Is there such a thing as exclusive ownership of symbols, names and culture among peoples whose territories and pasts are so intertwined?

This is why the new state has become an anthropological laboratory where two theories meet. One theory holds that the nation is natural and unchanging, something fixed and as hard as a stone; the other holds that nations are not only imagined but constructed communities that consist of many elements, sometimes even the same elements as neighboring countries—more like a puzzle or a sandwich than a solid stone block. In any case, a work in progress where component parts are constantly added and reshuffled, and where some people were first and some among the last to incorporate certain elements, similar to the states that resurfaced after the collapse of Yugoslavia, like Slovenia, Bosnia and Herzegovina, Croatia and Kosovo, all at various stages of creating their national identity. Elements built into these identities range from a fake past to mythology, from pure facts to pure inventions. But it seems that FYROM, in its nationalist fervor, surpassed them all when it came to the splendor and magnitude of its expensive kitsch.

Visual identity creates the first impression about who we are, or rather, in the case of Macedonia, it sends a strong message about who the country's population wants to be. To see the new look and the foundations of the new nation being created with my own eyes provided further motivation for my visit.

Because this nation, like my homeland, Croatia, is also a by-product of the collapse of Yugoslavia, I traveled burdened with anxiety. Did they know what they were doing? Had they not learned about the dangers of nationalism from the wars in Croatia,

in Bosnia and Herzegovina and in Kosovo in the early nineties?
And from the bloody ethnic cleansings of Muslims and genocide in
Srebrenica and the siege of Sarajevo, and tens upon tens of thousands of dead? One cannot forget about such fears, even in FYROM,
the republic from the former Yugoslavia that became independent
in a nonviolent way, without a war.

I met Ana at Macedonia Square, the central square in Skopje.
We rendezvoused beside a column some thirty meters tall bearing
the statue of a rider. The massive statue looks mighty and dominates the rather small square. Completed in 2011, the monument is
simply named *Equestrian Warrior*, although it is well known that
the bronze figure represents Alexander the Great on his rearing
horse Bucephalus. Before that I had walked in the vicinity, across
the old stone bridge over the Vardar River, which runs through the
middle of the city. There is another newly built square with an almost equally gigantic statue of Philip II (its official name is *Warrior*), also surrounded by other statues along with fountains and the
brand-new buildings of several museum and state institutions
adorned with Greek pillars and friezes.

I suppose that when a visitor who has little interest in history sees
the statues of Alexander and Philip, as well as the many smaller
statues of historical figures on the square, he might momentarily
have the impression that they are the remnants of some ancient Hellenistic town from two thousand years ago on which the new Skopje
was built. But on second glance even such a visitor can tell that the
statues are too new to be old and it would not come as a surprise to
learn that they were erected only within the last decade.

While waiting for Ana, I suddenly thought that the whole center
city looked like a Hollywood set that a film crew had abandoned in
a hurry.

Ana is in her midthirties, has a university education and owns a small building firm. I did not recognize her at all because she does not resemble Biljana. She is blondish with blue eyes, a bit shy at first. She was dressed informally in jeans and a jacket, looking like she could belong anywhere, as do other young people here. If anything, fashion has the capacity to unite them as a uniform might. We decided to sit outside; the weather that November of 2018 (the year is important because only a couple of months later the country changed its name and it was recognized by the Greeks) was still warm and pleasant.

I ordered a fruit salad, she an espresso. Here, even fruit salad has a history: when you order a mixed fruit salad as a dessert in a restaurant in France or Germany, you are probably not aware that in many countries it is known as a Macedonian salad. You could easily prepare it at home, the recipe is simple: take seasonal fruits, cut them up, add lemon juice and sugar and chill the bowl. The secret is the mixture of many ingredients, the more the better. It is generally considered an Italian dessert (although Italians never ventured as far as Macedonia when they invaded Albania during World War II). In Italy, *maccedonia di frutta* means a mixture of fruits. But here, should I order a Macedonian salad or just a fruit salad? What is the politically correct name nowadays? I asked. Ana laughed uneasily and to my surprise explained that "Macedonian salad" is mixed vegetables instead of fruits—it would be similar to what is known as a Greek salad in the rest of the world. Well, I ordered a fruit salad finally.

Ana seems not to be a very political or opinionated person. Maybe she is just too shy, I think, to voice her opinion in front of a virtual stranger, albeit a kind of distant relative. But when I ask her whether she considers herself a Macedonian, I see that she is no longer shy or insecure. Ana nods right away to confirm that she does. "What else could I be?" she asks. "My father was a Macedonian and so was my mother and their parents." Both her grandparents were born in the late thirties, just before World War II. Her ancestors must have belonged to the South Serbs, as they were called then. Does it take only three generations to, in a way, recreate a Macedonian nation and construct its national identity starting with ancient history?

So far, not only the new Skopje, but the story behind the name and the creation of a national identity reminds me of a historical epic. History is not on the side of Macedonian nationalists either for yet another reason: the migrations of the Slavs into Europe between the fifth and seventh centuries CE. The truth is that these newcomers overpowered most of the ancient tribes and peoples in the territories of the southeastern Balkans, which had already been assimilated under the Roman and Byzantine empires and, subsequent to that, the medieval Bulgarian and Serbian kingdoms—until the Ottomans conquered them and ruled up to the beginning of the twentieth century. The name Macedonia was preserved throughout history only as a geographical name for a territory, but "Macedonian" wasn't an ethnicity.

That territory was the last stronghold of the Ottomans in Europe as they were pushed out and nationalist movements exploded during the two Balkan wars and World War I. The Macedonian region was divided into three administrative regions and was not politically unified. Only at the turn of the twentieth century, the time of national movements in that part of Europe, does the name Macedonia pop up again. And it was only in 1944 that one of the republics of federal Yugoslavia was named Macedonia—the same name whose use Greece started to dispute in 1991.

Given the facts, it seems rather unreasonable to link today's population to the ancient tribe. It is as if Italians would claim a direct line to the old Romans or Swedes would conceive of themselves as the heirs of Vikings. But why should hard facts stand in the way of such a marvelous creation as a new-old nation? They are most certainly rarely an element of much importance in such political decision making.

Ana explained to me that she is aware of the link between the intense building activity and national identity, and of how both architecture and political propaganda are tinged with nationalism. But she didn't mind this and didn't mind being called a nationalist herself either. Only at that moment, for the first time, did she become surprisingly outspoken. "I am proud of being a Macedonian!" she declared, blushing a bit. "Before we were called Macedonians, but only in Yugoslavia. In Greece Macedonians are considered Greeks, in Bulgaria—Bulgarians. Now everyone else will have to recognize us as the Macedonian nation," she said with a broad smile. "Pride and dignity are important to me. . . ." I nodded hesitantly. But wouldn't it be better if the government got on with creating jobs and better living standards in a country where the average income of 350 euros is among the lowest in Europe? I asked. She did not seem to detect any connection here.

But what about the language, I wanted to know. My language is Macedonian, she insisted, knowing that Greeks oppose references to the language as Macedonian; in the Greek view, living in a specific territory does not automatically determine one's ethnicity.

Besides which, Greeks do not recognize the Macedonian minority in their own country and don't grant them minority rights either, just to make sure they do not get any ideas about independence and unification. Bulgarians, on the other hand, have always considered Macedonians as Bulgarians and their language as a dialect of Bulgarian. Many students from FYROM study in Bulgaria because of the similarities between the two country's languages. However, although Macedonian Cyrillic is somewhat different from the Bulgarian one, Macedonian was recognized as a separate language only in 1944. By the early 1990s, many Macedonians went to study in English at the American University in the southwest Bulgarian town of Blagoevgrad with a view to earning an internationally recognized degree.

When I asked a friend, a university professor in Skopje, whether she considered herself a Macedonian, she answered cautiously: "Do you mean a citizen of the state that includes the name? Or ethnic belonging?" She was making a distinction, the crucial distinction between the two notions. Apparently for many people this is not a simple question. It requires both historical and political elaboration. Her question sums up the entire spectrum of complications surrounding identity in this country where the name and ethnic belonging are both making political issues so divisive.

Although the big nationalist project cannot be accomplished without the support of people like my distant relative, not everybody is of the same opinion. Indeed, by negotiating with the Greeks, the Social Democratic and minority coalition government that came to power in May 2017 is trying to limit the damage done by the nationalists. In June 2018 the countries' respective prime ministers, Zoran Zaev and Alexis Tsipras, finally succeeded in signing the Prespa Accord concerning the new name of the Republic of North Macedonia. "This is our own rendezvous with history," said Tsipras. And perhaps the Greeks also fear that the FYROM's right to the name North Macedonia could now provide a pretense for mounting a claim to the Greek territory where Macedonians live. This is also a way for the renamed state to access associations and funds, join NATO and commence the EU accession talks that Greece had previously blocked.

When I looked out from the top floor of my hotel in the evening, I could see large imposing buildings with illuminated façades, avenues, bridges, squares—all basking in an electric glow. But in daylight, the picture was a bit different. In between the new buildings that house state institutions, museums and big corporations, there are smaller houses and streets, typical remnants of the architecture that emerged during more than five hundred years of Ottoman rule. It is as if, during the last decade or so, the new European town has been eating up the old Turkish one.

All these pristine white façades are newly built—sometimes directly onto an old building. Inventing the past does not end with fake "classical" Greek and other historicist statues. It involves other historical periods as well. From this point of view, Skopje becomes even more interesting. Many buildings incorporate a mixture of neoclassicism, art deco and even baroque elements, as if the architect could not decide which one to choose. Indeed, it could not have been easy, since none of these Western styles of architecture and art reached as far east as Skopje. After the Hellenistic, Roman and Byzantine periods, there were only the Ottomans and their architectural style; after World War II came communist urban planning. The new buildings are more concentrated on one side of the Vardar; on the other side of the river, communist-era buildings dominate. Among them, on one of the main streets running out of Macedonia Square, Arch Macedonia is a kind of Arc de Triomphe, as real as anything of this kind that you might see in Paris, Bucharest or Barcelona but erected only in 2012. These new buildings and façades, lampposts and bridges are more typical of eighteenth- and nineteenth-century Vienna and Paris—not Skopje. But they have intentionally been built to show that this town was not only a Turkish *čaršija* at the border of the empire. It was part of Europe—and therefore has the new-old buildings to prove it. The task of architecture here is to provide "proof" of the history that did not happen in Skopje—that is, to invent the truth.

Skopje is not the only example of this. The dictator Nicolae Ceausescu demolished half of old Bucharest in the late seventies to build elegant living quarters for his nomenclatura and his grandiose People's Palace, the world's second largest administrative building after the Pentagon. In 1703 Russian Tsar Peter the Great began building St. Petersburg from scratch on the shore of the Baltic Sea as proof of the same sense of European belonging.

There is not so much enthusiasm when it comes to dressing up socialist architecture, ugly gray blocks that, if nothing else, housed millions in quite decent conditions. These buildings are difficult to make over, to invest with any glamour. There are simply too many to be demolished, although their demolition is surely being considered. Socialist architecture is here to stay and represents the real rather than the invented past. Most of the buildings were constructed after July 1963, when a strong earthquake killed about a thousand people and left the majority of Skopje's citizens homeless. A famous Japanese architect, Kenzo Tange, was in charge of the city's reconstruction and some buildings from that time remain imposing today—the Central Post Office, skyscrapers of Karpoš and various institutions, as well as memorial buildings in the so-called brutalist style.

In charge of presenting the nationalist view of the past is a new riverside museum with an unusually long name: Museum of the Macedonian Struggle for Statehood and Independence, VMRO, and the Victims of the Communist Regime. The name itself indicates one intention of this project: to identify the nationalist party VMRO with the struggle for independence and ignore its history in ex-Yugoslavia. The museum is housed in a spacious building, one of many adorning the banks of the green Vardar. It is a curious place, a bit weird and sometimes scary. Wax figures of important people, scenes of torture as seen in horror movies. Covering the twentieth century, with the greater part dedicated to the birth of a national awareness and the desire for independence, it celebrates the Ilinden Uprising against the Turks in 1903. The rebels' Kruševo Republic, the first attempt at an autonomous Macedonia, lasted only ten days. But it was a clear sign that times were changing. As Turkish territory in Europe shrank and as Turks withdrew under Western military pressure, the great mixture or *maccedonia* of peoples living there fought for national independence, as the Ottoman and Austro-Hungarian empires started to crumble.

Visiting this museum and coming from the former Yugoslavia as I do, I saw that something was missing: a whole chapter on World War II, when Macedonian antifascist fighters joined Tito's forces and formed a common government in 1944. Josip Broz Tito was a commander of the army that fought Nazi occupation of Yugoslavia and later the president of the communist party, a statesman and the president of the country until his death in 1980. But the next fifty years in Yugoslavia are presented somewhat timidly too, without giving them the importance they deserve. A few photos and notes on the wall, a prison cell containing a political dissident and a room with wax figures of Tito and other comrades in the huge 6500-square-meter museum do not do justice to that period at all. For example, in the Kingdom of Yugoslavia, Macedonians were called Southern Serbs. But Tito was the man who, as if by magic, turned a geographical area into a nation and a federal republic by recognizing the Macedonian republic in 1944. It was thanks to this that the dream of the nation and independence became somewhat more real under communism and that the republic became an independent state in 1991 as the Socialist Federal Republic of Yugoslavia collapsed and the Yugoslav wars broke out (though peace held in Macedonia throughout).

Is it not curious that the period during which the place was part of Yugoslavia, despite being one of great benefits for the people living there, is totally marginalized? I asked a young museum guide, a historian. Why does the communist period receive such a small place in the museum? Obviously not used to questions from visitors, most of whom are schoolchildren and foreigners, the young man said that perhaps this is because it is only "a fragment in the long history of Macedonians." However, if the museum mostly focuses on a single hundred-year section of that "long history," then almost half of that period may well deserve more than just one room, I thought. This must come down to simple opportunism: the region flourished during communism, but communism is something not to be mentioned today. Not only in Macedonia, but in all of former communist Eastern Europe, it is difficult to mention the merits of communism, a system that, in a short time, brought modernization and changed an agrarian society into an urbanized, industrial one. It meant general education as well as the emancipation of women; this has to be recognized, even though such changes were accomplished by a totalitarian regime. And it is in this period and not before that Skopje, previously a small town at the border of the Ottoman Empire, became the urban capital of the Macedonian republic and, later on, of a nation-state with a problematic name.

During the best part of fifty years, several generations of people grew up as Macedonians in the Yugoslav Socialist Republic of Macedonia. It seems to be a small step from accepting this fact to believing themselves to be descendants of an ancient Macedonian tribe and even of Alexander the Great, if it is taken for granted that no direct historical continuity can be established. However, if we accept that nations are "imagined communities," a concept that Benedict Anderson developed in his 1983 book on the subject, then the story of a nascent nation looks just as it should: the imagined community of Macedonians wanted to give the name Macedonia to their new independent state. They are living proof of that geo-historical name. Add some other necessary ingredients like myth, emotions and imagination, and with some political and financial effort a new nation can even be constructed in twenty-first-century Europe: the first new nation of "Macedonians."

To be sure, most of these people are Christian Orthodox. This is confirmed by the Millennium Cross built in 2002 on Mount Vodno, a monument more than twice the height of the *Equestrian Warrior* that is also illuminated at night. When darkness falls, that bright cross lingers over Skopje as if suspended from the sky. At the same time, closer to the ground, the muezzin's singsong call to prayer wanders in the streets. This reminds Macedonians that they are not

alone, that Albanians, many of whom are Muslim, form the biggest
minority living here, accounting for some 25 percent of the population.

There are a fruit dessert, a territory and an ancient kingdom, all
of which go by the name of Macedonia. And a state as well, even if
it was a long and testing path from the geographical region to, as
of January 2019, its new name: Republic of North Macedonia. But
the job is far from finished. And its outcome hangs in the balance,
pending the support for the government of the Albanian minority,
which has its own demands and conditions. In 2001 Albanian in-
surgents attacked a police outpost and the ensuing conflict, which
lasted for much of the rest of the year, left tens of people dead. It was
the banning of the Albanian flag and the repression of the Albanian language that sparked first protests and then military conflict.
Nowadays, Albanians in Macedonia rightly view every expression
of Macedonian nationalism in the country with skepticism and fear.
One nationalism feeds the other and this is why it is so dangerous.

Macedonia fits well into the new picture of a nationalist Europe.
Precisely because of right-wing nationalism, among other things,
here in Skopje a nationalism akin to the one that created Italy and
France over the centuries is now giving birth to yet another nation-
state. Only that, being late to the construction site, the orchestra-
tors imagine that they have exclusive rights to the building blocks
of history and don't want to share them. But this is a disadvantage
that you simply have to endure if you are operating today rather
than a hundred years ago.

Ana and I parted amiably after discussing matters of family inheritance. We obviously did not agree on the subject of Macedonia and its history and name, but why should we?

After all, the giant cross and the penetrating voice of the muezzin waking me before dawn live in peaceful coexistence now.

Today one can visit Skopje, sit on Macedonia Square, look at the fake Greek sculptures and equally fake neoclassical buildings, Parisian bridges and lampposts, enjoy the sun and be reminded of the history of this country, both real and invented, everywhere you look. But perhaps precisely because of these views, one becomes increasingly aware that both Macedonian and Greek national identity—as well as any other, be it old or new—is a construction.

In Skopje, fact and fiction merge in a kitschy but in some respects moving, albeit nationalistic narrative of people looking for something to be proud of. It is not moving because of the political drive to create a nation, but because of those people to whom national identity, even if it is a construct, means something of which they feel proud.

At the same time this is a state that is hoping to become part of the EU, a large union to which it would have to delegate a part of its sovereignty. But nobody seems to notice this paradox, at least not at the moment.

A Parrot in Sweden, and Other Immigrant Issues

*On old immigrants
and new refugees*

visited Sweden for the first time in 1970, on a student visa that allowed me to work for three months. It was a long train journey to the north, two days and two nights. First, from Zagreb to East Berlin, where my then husband and I stayed with a student for one night. We did not know him, but our friend back home in Zagreb, who had traveled to Sweden several times before on this cheap route, gave us his address.

Back then, Germany was still a divided country and it was illegal to stay in the German Democratic Republic without registering with the police, so our host took a risk having us in his house. The train arrived late at night and the one for the ferry to Sweden left in the early hours, so he had rightly figured that the neighbors would not notice his visitors. We left at dawn with a loaf of dark bread that his mother had baked for us and two bottles of water. The shops were closed at that early hour and anyway, we had no East German currency.

The journey through Sweden seemed endless and took us through forests that were dotted only here and there with wooden cottages and a few mansions, all painted red. Stockholm's central station, however, looked like a glamorous shopping mall compared with the railway station in East Berlin. We exchanged some West German marks for Swedish kronas and bought tickets for a local bus to a suburb of Stockholm—where Thomas was waiting for us. He was the Swedish friend we had met the year before in Zagreb. At that time many young Swedes and West Germans were hitchhiking along our Adriatic coast, curious to see firsthand what communism looked like in Yugoslavia. Thomas had found us a room to rent and jobs in a warehouse of the big department store Åhlén & Holm. We were to stack shelves. It was well-paid work and we calculated that, back home, we could live for a whole year on the money we saved. The next day our Swedish friend accompanied us to the police headquarters to get us work visas and tax ID numbers. We were set to start working the next day.

As of now, we were "temporary workers."

We were surprised at how smoothly the paperwork was processed at the police station and the warehouse. Back home in Zagreb there were endless queues at police headquarters, where we had to kill time, answer hostile questions and collect stamps and missing signatures. This often involved coming back a second or even a third time. Swedes were kind and willing to help, whether policemen, shopkeepers, bus drivers or anyone in the street. We spoke English, which was the key to feeling comfortable and welcomed, because almost everyone we met already spoke English fluently. In less than a week, we felt at home in the suburb. Our co-workers were mostly Finns, very diligent and taciturn people when not drinking and fighting among themselves with knives, as was occasionally the case; however, since they did not show any desire to socialize, it was easy to avoid them.

There were only two drawbacks: the weather and the price of food. We arrived in early June and back in Zagreb, some two thousand kilometers to the south, spring was already giving way to summer. But up here it was cold; at 50°F winter didn't yet seem over to us, despite the brilliant sunshine. The mystery of the light windbreakers that everyone wore, looking as if they were ready to perform some sort of sport, was finally revealed to me and I learned not to leave home without one. As soon as a cloud covered the sun, the temperature would suddenly drop several degrees, just as it did when we were caught in a sudden shower. Then summer came, at least the Swedes told us so, but it did not turn out to be much better: 68°F compared with 86°F in our part of Europe.

Shopping was even more of a problem because the food was very expensive for us. I was astonished at the price of tomatoes or slices of watermelons in plastic wrap. We were used to buying a whole big watermelon of five or more kilos. When we were children, we ate them on the beach, first chilling them in the sea. Mother would cut the melon and give us a huge piece that we had to hold with both hands. We would eat it while the sweet juice ran down our hands, chins and even tummies. But in Stockholm, our kind of food was considered exotic and was therefore more expensive. The Swedes had excellent and cheap fruits of their own, like wild strawberries and blueberries, as well as fish of all kinds, but bigger, fatter and less salty than the fish from the Mediterranean. They also had delicious young potatoes, which turned out to be the staple of our diet that summer. There was however one thing that we could not get used to: the strict controls on alcohol. For somebody coming from a Mediterranean country, it was ridiculous to have to go to a special shop to buy wine, as if it were a poisonous liquid and not part of a normal dinner.

We kept working on Saturdays for extra money. Sundays were free for excursions to Stockholm, which was about forty-five minutes away on a bus that ended at the very center. This beautiful city on the waterfront, principally built on a small number of islands, also attracted me because of its narrow streets and old buildings, reminding me of similar Mediterranean towns at home. We enjoyed long walks through the medieval town Gamla Stan, situated on a tiny island. On a nice day the reflections of yellow and brownish façades would flicker on the surface of the water, giving it a surreal glow. After passing the bridge close to the huge Royal Palace on the way to the opera house, we would walk along the waterfront all the way to yet another small island covered with dark green trees and caressed by the sea breeze.

The city was new and foreign to me, but not strange. I felt like I had in Milan or Vienna or any other big European city I had visited before. Although it was so far north, the cultural habits and references were the same. On the way back home to Solna in the afternoon, we used to sit in a small coffeehouse where American draft dodgers congregated; in order to avoid being sent to Vietnam, between 60,000 and 100,000 young men had left the United States for Canada and Sweden. Over cheap, bad coffee that you could refill and cake—my favorite was a *kanelbulle* (a cinnamon bun)—we would talk to them not so much about politics, but about music. These young Americans were fascinated that we, coming from a communist country, listened to the same music they did: Joan Baez and Bob Dylan, Peter, Paul and Mary, Pink Floyd.

For them, all communist countries were the same.

If someone had told me then that I would end up living in Stockholm twenty-five years later, I would not have believed them. Back then, there were things that I could not have believed would happen, starting with the fact that my homeland, Yugoslavia, would no longer exist in 1991. However, I came to live in Stockholm again not as a war refugee or an economic migrant, but rather as a "love migrant," even if there is no such category. I married a Swedish journalist I met while he was reporting on the wars in Yugoslavia. Stockholm became my city, more dazzling to me than before. You appropriate a city when you find your own café, bookstore, hairdresser, favorite streets and, of course, friends. I no longer felt like a visitor. Swedes themselves made it easier for me, because they did not have a complex about being in or from the very center of Europe; they did not look suspiciously at those who came from outside, as if to imply that outsiders belonged to the periphery. The Swedes saw themselves as being on the margins; they talked about Europe as "the continent" or about "going down to Europe," as if they were not really part of it themselves.

Again, I had the same feeling that life here was well organized and that the institutions of the state were there to help you, not to harass or supervise you. As a citizen, you must fulfill only one important condition: you have to pay your taxes regularly. Fully and regularly. All your privileges derive from your tax ID number. Or rather, you do not exist until you have one. To my great surprise, I discovered that I already had one—it was the same number that I had received twenty-five years before. This was proof of having a proper labor status. I was deeply impressed. At that time, Croatia was experiencing its postwar transition to democracy, which predictably resulted in chaos, especially when it came to issuing official documents. For example, in addition to the old Yugoslav personal numbers, citizens of the new state were now issued with new ones—but they were not considered valid without the old ones. Still, it would be unfair to compare these two very different countries. Not least because in Sweden I did not live the life of an economic migrant, a "guest worker," or *Gastarbeiter* (the German term became habitual in the sixties), but of a freelance writer who was not forced to look for a job. This was of course a privilege but also a kind of handicap: there was no need for me to learn the language. In my walk of life and in the company of rather international friends, everyone spoke English.

My only complaint was, and still is, that you have to go to a special store to buy a simple bottle of wine.

I did not meet many people from my part of the world, although this was the time when the refugees hit hardest by the Yugoslav wars came to Sweden in great numbers, especially from Bosnia and Herzegovina. One day, by chance, I overheard the owner of a flower shop I had entered speaking to someone on the telephone. He was speaking Serbian. His language sounded a bit rusty. Marko, as he introduced himself, belonged to one of the earlier waves of migration in which a lot of Greek, Italian and later Yugoslav workers, mostly single men, arrived in Sweden. Many married Swedish women and did not return home.

Marko had his own flower shop. A dark, short, stocky man, he was always in a good mood and treated visitors more like old friends who just happened to drop in. I enjoyed visiting him occasionally to chat in what we called "our language," which for political reasons had now been split in two and was no longer called Serbo-Croatian. Marko was a real gentleman. He gave me a rose every time I called by.

When he spoke about the life he led before coming to Sweden, he did not sound nostalgic. He was born in a province deep in Serbia, where he spent his adolescence. When he was conscripted to the army and sent to the barracks in Belgrade, Marko saw the world beyond the hills and pastures for the first time. And he liked it—he loved the asphalted streets instead of mud, the solid apartment buildings instead of village huts, the well-dressed people, the trams, the cars, the cinemas and the cafés.

After his two years of military service in the capital, and also of watching movies and football games and sitting in an ice cream parlor with his pals or in a park drinking beer and looking at the girls on Sunday afternoons, Marko decided not to return to his village. But there was no job in Belgrade for a young peasant with no schooling. Equipped with an address on a piece of paper, he landed in Stockholm. After just a few days he had his first job. His new life in the Swedish fairy tale had begun.

In that fairy tale he learned Swedish, met a local blond girl and fell in love with her. They married and had two children, a boy and a girl. I do not know how he came up with the idea to open a flower shop, but it soon became a success story; he could count celebrities and even a member of the royal family among his customers. Their photos with a smiling Marko were proudly displayed, pinned to the wall at the counter. "Thanks Marko, the flowers were magnificent!" He and his wife worked day and night in the shop; for a couple of weeks every year, usually in the winter, they joined a cruise that called in at Venice, Dubrovnik and other historical sites around the Mediterranean. Sipping his whiskey on the upper deck, dressed in a white dinner jacket and smoking a fat cigar, Marko had left the backwaters of Serbia far behind him and was now the incarnation of success. He also visited his mother every few years and sent her money, never regretting that he had left his village and Yugoslavia.

I envied him because he seemed to me totally integrated in Swedish society, even assimilated. I couldn't say the same thing about myself. I sometimes felt like an outsider because of the language, of small things I failed to get right, even if only a cake recipe on the flour bag or the instructions for operating a sophisticated corkscrew. Once I found myself without electricity because I did not understand a warning taped to the entrance door announcing a power cut due to repairs being carried out in our building. These things improved with time. Still, in my eyes, Marko was far better adapted to life in Sweden than I was.

Yet nobody's life is a fairy tale. His children married and left home. A few years ago, his wife died and he was left alone with Miki, a big *Ara* parrot who had lived in a cage in the flower shop since a point in time long before we met. When Miki was not asleep, he would greet visitors with a shriek. But more often than not Miki would slowly and solemnly walk back and forth on the perch in his cage, looking at you with one eye, then turn his head and scrutinize you with the other.

Miki was Marko's only companion now. One day a policeman entered the shop; some animal lover had denounced Marko for keeping the bird there. The policeman was none too pleased about being there, because he was a cherished customer too. But as it happened, keeping Miki in the shop was not against the law so long as the cage with the bird in it was not kept in a highly visible place in order to attract customers—the commercial use of pets in

Sweden is forbidden. Nonetheless, despite Miki's living in the back room, the policeman was not satisfied. The birdcage was too small. According to a 2014 law, Miki had to have a cage of at least 13 meters (square or cubic, Marko was not sure). And that was not all. In order for the bird not to feel lonely, the law entitled Miki to a minimum of six hours of company. Or to a partner—i.e., another bird.

Marko was rather astonished at such strict rules to protect pets, wondering if anyone actually checked whether children had big enough rooms or if they were lonely. But he was not too worried, because he was keeping Miki company for at least twelve hours every day; what they did not do was sleep together. All Marko had to do was pay a fine of about four hundred dollars and promise to buy a bigger cage. Thereafter, he forgot about the unpleasant incident. The police did not forget, however; a few months later a policewoman came to check on Miki's situation. As it had not improved, Marko had to pay a fine again. This time he had to promise the policewoman that Miki would also get a heat lamp. She had decided that the room was too cold for the parrot, even though it was clearly warm enough for a human being. But Marko did not want to get into a discussion with her about animal rights versus human rights—he just wanted her to leave. When the police came the third time, they did not bother to fine him again—they just took Miki away, together with his cage that was allegedly much too small.

"You have been warned twice but still not fulfilled the conditions for keeping the bird," one of them said. Marko's eyes filled with tears as he told me the story. "Doesn't love for the animal count at all?" he asked them, but to no avail. The last he heard of Miki was his shriek, as if calling Marko for help.

Once Miki was gone, there was nobody to talk to except his customers. Good, but not good enough. His children would call him from time to time, he would call his elderly mother back home, but he felt more and more lonely and depressed. One day Marko woke up at home with his leg red and swollen under the knee. It was so painful that he could barely stand, let alone walk on it. He had to hire an assistant to help him in the flower shop. But he did not visit a doctor, he just waited for the pain to pass. After a week the leg looked even worse. Never in his whole life had he visited a doctor and he did not intend to do so now, probably not even if it were a matter of life and death. And anyway, this was only some sort of infection that would soon pass.

Marko had departed from his village long ago, but he not entirely left it behind. Part of him was still there: far from health checks, scientific medicine, nurses in white aprons and sterilized towels. When his daughter came and saw his condition, she immediately took him to hospital despite his grumbling and, ultimately, angry protests. He made it just in time to survive the sepsis, but both of his kidneys had failed and Marko had to start dialysis.

He sank from lethargy into depression.

Then the cat killed his mother. The mother was very old, over ninety, but healthy. She had been living alone and preparing her own food on a stove fueled by wood that she chopped up herself with an ax. Then she happened to step on her house cat. If only the cat had not bitten her foot! The wound would not heal, no traditional herbal medicine helped. Marko was not surprised when in a telephone conversation his mother told him that a neighbor had taken her to hospital in the nearest town, where she was told that an amputation was necessary. Were it not carried out, his mother would die. Over the phone, the doctor in charge asked Marko in Stockholm to allow them to amputate the leg, but he refused.

"My mother would rather die than to live with only one leg. She doesn't want to be a cripple," he told me later. According to Marko one had to understand the old woman. She lived alone, but after an amputation she would have to move to a home for the elderly. Changing her life completely at over ninety years of age in order to live a year or two longer did not make much sense.

She was kept in the local hospital, where she soon died.

To me, it seemed very much like a cultural rather than a medical problem. Only after he told me about his decision did I realize that while, on the one hand, he was more a part of Swedish culture than me, on the other, I was better adapted to city life, in spite of my poor language skills. He was a child of a village, whereas I was born and bred in a city. Moving from one city to another, from Rijeka to Zagreb to Stockholm, was in many ways difficult because of different habits and ways of doing things there, but still somehow the same. The clash between rural and urban culture that Marko had to cope with was greater than that between two cities located two thousand kilometers apart. This made my life in Stockholm so much easier than Marko's. To visit a doctor when you are ill is a mere reflex of urban cultural behavior—thus I would have imagined that more than forty years in a city would have been enough to stop him fearing a visit to the doctor, as if he were still the small village boy of yesterday.

Though Marko had not completely integrated, his children had grown up as urban Swedes and could visit a hospital without thinking twice. Neither of them spoke Serbian, which Marko had never tried to teach them. He was too busy at work. And why teach them another small language that they would never have a chance to use?

"Sometimes I regret it, but sometimes I think it was better like that, better for them," he reflected, now sitting alone in his shop, greeting customers and waiting for a suitable kidney donor.

Shortly after the war in Bosnia and Herzegovina ended in 1995, I became acquainted with a Bosniak family, the Fazlics, who had come to Sweden as refugees. In the case of most Muslims from Bosnia—and in contrast to others (from Serbia or Croatia)—"Muslim" indicates ethnic and not necessarily religious belonging. For that reason "Muslim" was later changed to "Bosniak." Almost 100,000 refugees from Bosnia and Herzegovina arrived in Sweden, of whom 75,000 asked for asylum.

The mother and father, Faruk and Alma, were in their fifties; they had two grown daughters. The older one was already married and had a small girl of her own. The Swedish state put the family up in a furnished three-room apartment in a suburban part of Stockholm, a mixed area where native Swedes also lived. All they needed to do independently was to buy a satellite dish so they could watch TV channels from back home. They also got an allowance of about nine dollars per person per day.

When I met Faruk and Alma, they had been already waiting for two years to be granted asylum. It was difficult to live in such suspense—most of all for Faruk, who had a university degree and had worked in a local administrative post back home. He found it humiliating to live jobless; he felt helpless, a burden to his family and to society. While the authorities review their case, a process that can last for years, asylum seekers are allowed to work but only under special conditions. Faruk killed time by smoking and watching TV programs from home ("home" was everything down south, not only Bosnia where he came from, but the entire ex-Yugoslavia). This depressed him even more. Occasionally he would go out to meet a few fellow countrymen in the neighborhood.

Faruk didn't even try to learn Swedish and often suffered from various ailments. The family could not help him and the fissure between them grew.

His wife, Alma, who had been a housewife, quickly learned the language; Swedish courses were free, but not obligatory. Somebody had to manage their daily routines, from going to school meetings and assisting the younger daughter or their granddaughter, to shopping, doctors' visits or making phone calls when practical issues popped up. The roles of mother and father suddenly reversed. Now Alma was the one who was in charge, who took responsibility for the family.

It took several years for the Swedish authorities to reach a positive decision on their application for asylum. Indeed, the Bosnian war refugees who were granted asylum were to prove exemplary as some of society's best integrated migrants, like many of the refugees who came to Sweden before them: Jews before and after World War II, Hungarians after the revolution of 1956, Czechs after the Prague Spring and their country's occupation by Soviet-led forces in the summer of 1968. They were Europeans from a similar background and culture; generally much better educated than non-European refugees, but this is not politically correct to mention. Many of them made careers as translators, theater directors and even politicians.

One of those refugees was Aida Hadžialić, who came to Sweden with her parents when she was five and went on to become a lawyer and, in 2014, minister of education for the Social Democratic Party. Twenty-seven when she was appointed, she was by far the youngest minister in the government. Research confirms that this particular group integrated within one generation, which is considered an extraordinary success. However, merely to voice a dilemma over whether Sweden could integrate Afghans or Somalis today as it had Bosnians two decades before is to risk accusations of racism.

Refugees from Bosnia looked just like Swedes and did not feel the stigma of being recognized as foreigners, at least not at first sight. The skin color of refugees is never mentioned in Sweden; it is ignored on purpose. Everyone behaves as if it does not matter. The minister of culture, Alice Bah Kuhnke, has a Gambian father. The color of her skin did not matter, the skin color of many others who came earlier did not matter either. But the question still remains: Could this change once the majority of refugees entering Sweden have a different skin color? When does prejudice kick in and color start playing a role? Or is it not a question of numbers, but rather of how much taxpayers' money is spent on them? Or is prejudice about something completely different?

Then came 2015 and 2016 and the new wave of migration of more than two million people from outside Europe entering the European Union. Many of them reached Sweden and, according to the Organization for Economic Cooperation and Development, 163,000 applied for asylum in 2015 alone. It means that Sweden, with a population of around 10.2 million people, took by far the most refugees per capita in the EU.

The year before this large immigration wave began, two authors, Karl-Olov Arnstberg and Gunnar Sandelin, wrote a book entitled *Invandring och mörkläggning* (*Immigration and Blackout*). When the book was first published, it was completely ignored by the media, confirming the two authors' view that the truth about immigration is indeed covered up as the result of a tacit conspiracy between the political elite and the media. Arnstberg and Sandelin decided to challenge this—out of their own pockets, they paid for a full-page advertisement in the country's biggest quality newspaper that listed eight facts about immigration from official statistics quoted in their book. For instance, in the period between 2000 and 2013 Sweden gave over 1.1 million immigrants residence permits. By 2014 Sweden granted 16,400 Syrians asylum whereas, between them, Denmark, Norway and Finland granted it to only a few thousand Syrians. But perhaps most shocking of all was this: people born abroad, who make up about 15 percent of the population, had benefited from 60 percent of the country's income support.

The authors were accused of xenophobia and racism; a moralistic discussion immediately broke out and very few defended Arnstberg and Sandelin. In fact, a considerable number of the newspaper's readers criticized the editorial board for having published the ad. The facts had been published but still ignored.

The Swedish government, led by the Conservatives up until 2014, and then by the Social Democrats, preferred to bury the facts generated by its own office of statistics. When the great wave of refugees rolled in during 2015, Sweden continued to play the role of the "moral champion of the world."

On the surface, no changes were immediately visible. As before, the government's immigration policy was not publicly disputed. Neither the media nor ordinary people expressed any concern about, say, the risks of overstretching the welfare system. The first sign of a change of heart was reflected in opinion polls showing the rapid rise in popularity of the Sweden Democrats, a far-right party that had barely featured in the national parliamentary elections of 2010, with just 5.7 percent of the vote. In the general election of 2018, it received 17.5 percent and suddenly became the country's third largest party. This was achieved purely by concentrating on an anti-immigrant, anti-EU message, just as other far-right parties had done throughout Europe, in countries such as Germany, Austria, France, Italy and Denmark. One could claim that the Sweden Democrats are a result of the Swedish Social Democrats having chosen to ignore the problem of refugees and asylum seekers for decades during the twentieth century, when they were in power.

Within a relatively short time, societies in Sweden and elsewhere in Europe have switched from open to closed, from welcoming refugees to firmly rejecting them. In an opinion poll published by the Swedish newspaper *Aftonbladet*, the proportion of respondents showing willingness to help refugees had fallen from 54 percent in 2015 to 30 percent in 2016. During the same period, the number of those in favor of taking fewer asylum seekers almost doubled, from 34 percent to 60 percent.

It has slowly dawned upon Swedes that immigration is expensive, that social funds really have to be shared with people who do not contribute by paying taxes and will not do so for quite some time to come, certainly not before they start to work. Researchers suggest that this can take years, especially for those with no education.

In 2017 Hungarian Prime Minister Viktor Orbán said in one of his many xenophobic speeches, "Now the Muslim communities coming to Europe see their own culture, their own faith, their own lifestyles and their own principles as stronger and more valuable than ours. So, whether we like it or not, in terms of respect for life, optimism, commitment, the subordination of individual interests and ideals, today Muslim communities are stronger than Christian communities. Why would anyone want to adopt a culture that appears to be weaker than their own strong culture? They won't, and they never will! Therefore re-education and integration based on re-education cannot succeed. [. . .] Over the next few decades the main question in Europe will be this: Will Europe remain the continent of the Europeans?"

On the other hand, new immigrants and refugees feel the change in atmosphere too. They are settled in enclaves or ghettos, where more and more drug-related crime, honor killing, violence and rapes are reported, especially in the south of Sweden, where the majority of refugees and asylum seekers live.

One of the few sources of hope for change is urban life itself. Life in a city changes people; it imprints itself on your personality, even changing your identity. Urbanization is also a process of individualization and the shedding of former habits and rules. However, many new refugees in Europe are facing a barrier that few refugees faced before: they all come from a non-European culture. Still, perhaps the fact that they are overwhelmingly Muslims would not have been decisive when it came to perceptions of them had it not been for the series of terrorist attacks in Paris, Nice, Brussels, Manchester, Stockholm and other cities, attacks committed exclusively by Muslim extremists, some of them born to immigrant parents. These crimes stigmatized a whole population; Muslim immigrants have carried the burden of being potentially violent people, primitive and unable—or even unwilling—to integrate.

Marko's case and the experience of a previous generation of immigrants seem ideal compared with what new immigrants are having to face. But if even Marko did not integrate completely in almost fifty years of life in Sweden, then how will new refugees from the Middle East and Africa adapt to life in their new homeland? What about their "parrots" and other issues that are important to them, bound to cause misunderstandings?

I recently visited the Fazlic family in their spacious apartment in Jakobsberg on the outskirts of Stockholm, the same one that the Swedish authorities assigned them in the 1990s, even before any decision was made about whether they could stay. Coming out of the subway station, I found myself on a small square with a supermarket, a few more shops and a café. What was unusual, however, were some thirty dark-skinned men, both young and old, standing in small groups, smoking, gesticulating, immersed in a lively and loud discussion in unfamiliar languages. A few women I saw had their heads covered or were dressed in chadors, one pushing a pram, others carrying heavy bags full of food. The square did not look as if it was in Stockholm or anywhere in Europe, at least not as we like to imagine it. Faruk waited for me in the square.

"Newcomers," he said in a dry, matter-of-fact way. "Our old neighborhood is changing.

"Many of our people from Bosnia went back. And now we have these new refugees moving in, mostly from Africa and the Middle East. The worst are those from Somalia. They have very, very different habits," Faruk said, although he did not go into detail. Perhaps in order not to be misinterpreted. "I know that they have a hard time adjusting, but they should at least show some respect and gratitude for all that they receive in this country," he added, pointing at the litter around us and at the neglected children's playground. Faruk was obviously speaking as an experienced "former" refugee. "But I don't think that Swedes mind the color of their skin as much as their different behavior."

Nobody knows better than Faruk how long it takes, regardless of where you come from, to become part of Swedish society—even if you already live here. After all, he himself had not managed to "arrive" yet, not even after two and a half decades. Then he suddenly stopped and made a gesture toward the houses surrounding us. It was the middle of the day and the windows were shut with no signs of life behind them. At this time of day the people were probably all at work; Faruk shook his head.

Swedes live in these apartment buildings too, he said. "Imagine, my family and I have a flat as big as theirs although we don't pay a cent for it as I don't work. And for the satellite dish on my balcony, I can't pay for that either and my Swedish neighbors know that. . . . I only regret I was too old for employment once I got my papers in order. And I am endlessly grateful to the Swedes for taking us in when we were fleeing the war. But believe me, it can't go on like this. I see that our Swedish neighbors are getting tired of us refugees, I can feel it. The state should provide us with a better chance to work and pay back what we got, not let us live on social benefits. Besides, nobody likes to live from charity."

My Favorite Card

*The cracks in a
magic piece of plastic*

My favorite plastic card is not a golden credit card or an exclusive membership card, although it feels just like that.

Gray-blue with white fields for name, surname, date of birth, personal or social security number, issuing institution, card number and expiration date—my favorite card has a modest appearance. In the upper-right-hand corner there are two letters, indicating a country, in a circle of stars. This is my European health insurance card, or EHIC. Carte Vitale, Tessera Sanitaria, EHIC UK (for the time being!), Europska Kartica Zdravstvenog Osiguranja—the local name does not matter as long as it means the same and signifies the health insurance card, which can be used in all EU member states as well as in non-EU states of Iceland, Liechtenstein, Norway and Switzerland. It entitles you to emergency medical assistance in state hospitals under the same conditions as residents of the country you are visiting—for free or for a small charge, depending on the local rules. Needless to say, when I got it, it was life changing.

For years I needed hemodialysis three times a week—a costly procedure of filtering blood through a big machine in lieu of my kidneys, which did not work. I understood that in cases like mine, you could not even get medical insurance in the United States if you had a preexisting condition. Paying between $250 and $350 per dialysis (I needed three a week and the money was contributed by my friends) during a visit to the States in the 1980s, I learned to appreciate the national health services I used in Europe, services that sometimes even verged on going too far, both in former Yugoslavia and in Sweden.

Once when I traveled to a conference in Washington, D.C., as a Swedish citizen, boxes and boxes of liquids for dialysis awaited me in my hotel. Then I was on another kind of dialysis that did not involve any kind of machine but required four two-liter packs of special liquid per day; it was called peritoneal dialysis, a special kind of blood filtration through the peritoneum or a stomach membrane. To cover my four-day stay, thirty-two liters were therefore duly flown in and deposited in my room, all at the expense of the Swedish health service. The room was not big and I had to maneuver my way to the bathroom quite carefully. But this did not bother me of course. I was grateful. On another occasion a truck of liquid with a monthly supply—more than a hundred liters—arrived in the Croatian village where I intended to stay for a holiday. It was overwhelming and moving to see a truck climbing the narrow hilly road to the village some 150 kilometers from the nearest liquid storage facility somewhere in Italy. You have to wonder how that was possible, how much it cost Swedish taxpayers for me to enjoy my holidays abroad. However, these things have nothing to do with the "magic" of the EHIC card; both of them happened before the card was even invented, and are simply the benefits of a rich country's public health insurance plan.

Yes, a country has to be rich to cater to the "luxury" needs of such a patient, because in spite of the same principle of national insurance, Croatia could not have afforded to proceed in the same way. But there are very few patients like me who fly from one continent to another for work, who travel back and forth between countries or take holidays abroad. Since dialysis and other such sophisticated services are so costly, and some countries do not even seem to have sufficient resources to support the people among their own populations who need it, health services invest in improving organ transplants, given that these are cheaper by comparison and give more freedom of movement to patients. I was lucky to get a kidney transplant and, at the same time, lower the costs to the service.

Sweden, one example among many, is key to how the "magic card" works—which is to say that the EHIC stands upon the pillars of state-run national insurance plans. In one way or another, medical insurance is usually obligatory for every citizen of a European country and, for the majority of people, publicly funded through taxation. By linking all twenty-eight national health systems together (or twenty-seven after Brexit) where emergencies are concerned, the European Union only makes use of what was already available on a national basis.

But I know other people who have learned to appreciate this card too.

A good friend of mine experienced a near fatal incident on a summer holiday in Italy a few years ago. As a tourist, trying to see as much as possible in the time you have can be fairly demanding on your health, even when you are young. Jan was in his late fifties but also a keen cyclist and in a good condition. He and his wife, Anika, left their hotel in Rome rather early one day and went to see the ruins of the Forum, figuring that it would be better to visit museums later on. Then they would at least be protected from the heat, which could become unbearable in August. It was eleven o'clock and already hot when they decided to take a bus to their next destination. While they waited, Jan's face suddenly went pale and sweat started pouring from his forehead. Worried, Anika made him sit down in a nearby café. He suddenly felt dizzy and nauseated, he said, followed by an unpleasant sensation in his chest. His wife did not wait for this to pass but called an ambulance.

In hospital Jan was diagnosed with a heart attack that required immediate intervention. He had two stents inserted and left the hospital the next day. The reason Jan now finds himself in my story actually has to do with a question that Anika was asked at the hospital admission office: What kind of health insurance does your husband have? Anika took out a bluish plastic EHIC card and her husband's picture ID. She was quite confident that his EHIC would cover the financial side of things. It was brand new and the first time he had needed to use it. This was a classic case of an emergency that required immediate intervention and the card was created especially for such situations. Anika was lucky because by this time hospitals in Rome had acquired sufficient experience of helping tourists. When foreigners started using it years before, it might be that the EHIC would be turned down and a credit card or private health insurance demanded instead. The patient would then have to pay the bill himself. The cost of the lifesaving procedure for Jan was considerable. But the hospital administrator accepted the card and the ID and made photocopies of both. Nothing further was required. It could not have been simpler.

The next summer, Tanja, a friend from Croatia, ended up in a Berlin hospital because of a blackout and temporary amnesia. All she remembers is that she suddenly lost consciousness in a hotel room. A female cleaner found her in a pool of blood. Tanja had hit the top of her head on the desk as she fell and received a cut. In the hospital doctors were not as concerned about the wound as they were about her blackout. Why would a healthy person in her sixties suddenly faint? Tanja had a series of neurological tests, along with an MRI scan of her brain. It turned out that she required a procedure to remove a blood clot. After two weeks she could leave the hospital, which was when the question of payment arose. Presented with the bill, she almost fainted again. But she remembered that I had some experience of German hospitals and called me. What should she do? The situation was easily solved. By that time, Croatia was already a member of the EU, but Tanja did not have her card with her. Her daughter couriered it to the hospital overnight.

Tanja was right to call me because of my experience of hospitals in several European countries, both those in which I lived and those to which I had traveled, as well as the United States. In my case, I need to have my EHIC with me at all times. While most people may never need it, I would feel very insecure traveling abroad without it. As the recipient of a kidney transplant, I am prone to infections as a result of my weak immune system. It is not often that I get them, but I have to be prepared. In fact, the card saved my life once. I had a very bad case of peritonitis, an inflammation that could lead to sepsis or blood poisoning if left untreated, and ended up in a hospital in Vienna as a Swedish EHIC patient.

Even within my circle of friends, I know of a few more cases in recent years that required the use of an EHIC. Robert broke his leg while skiing in Austria two years ago and received surgery in a hospital in Innsbruck on a Croatian EHIC. The father of another friend was visiting his daughter in Germany and needed emergency heart surgery, which was also carried out on a Croatian EHIC. Without this surgery, he would not have survived his trip back. Another friend, Carl, is a Swede who lives in Austria and has an Austrian EHIC. In the middle of an important conference that he had organized, he suddenly lost his sight in one eye and ended up in the hospital in Hamburg. After many tests and a few days there, he was diagnosed with a stroke that had affected his eyesight. Already in shock as a direct result of the incident, he (like others) received yet another shock when he saw the bill. Although he was not required to pay it himself, it was clear that if he had been responsible, he would have had to pay back the money he needed to borrow for the rest of his life!

Public health insurance is a uniquely European invention established in various countries at the beginning of the twentieth century, followed much later by Canada, Australia, Japan and New Zealand. It originated in the German Empire under Chancellor Otto von Bismarck when, in 1883, he made it obligatory for employers in industry to pay for the *Krankenversicherung* (sickness insurance) of low-income workers. A few years later Germany became the first country to introduce old-age insurance, a form of pension. Later on, both social-democratic and conservative governments collaborated on legislation to widen the scope of such measures until all citizens were able to benefit from them and no government would dare question them, at least so far. Since Bismarck's reform, the

EHIC is the most innovative—and important—contribution to public health.

This "magic card," which came fully into effect in 2006, is based on one's official country of residence (typically, the country in which you pay your taxes), not on citizenship. Therefore, in order to get one you need a tax ID number or social security number—or in any case proof that you are covered by a state welfare system, because that is where the bill for emergency health care is sent. The EHIC also covers health care required for preexisting chronic conditions such as kidney dialysis, oxygen therapy and chemotherapy.

By now, 40 percent of the population, or some 200 million people, in the EU have it.

It was possible to receive emergency help in a foreign country before 2006 too, but you had to take along a valid E111 form. After all, tourism was growing and health care abroad was also a necessity for the increasingly mobile workforce across the EU.

There are, however, differences between countries in getting the EHIC. In Romania, one must have been insured for the previous five years to be eligible for a card. Romania is also the only EU country where not all permanent residents are covered by health insurance; according to some statistics, only 85 percent of Romanians do, their insurance status linked to employment, family membership, social benefits or some other form of payment. Among the Roma minority there, the proportion of those insured is dramatically lower; most Roma are not entitled to national health care because they have no identity papers or no permanent residence (it is not uncommon for them to have neither). Therefore they do not have EHIC cards, which creates a problem when they migrate to another EU country. Physicians in Denmark and Sweden dealing with homeless Roma from Romania, for example, recommend that the EU ensure the EHIC is universally accessible and not subject to national requirements such as employment or residency. But the fact remains that, at the end of the day, a poor country like Romania has to pay for the care that citizens receive abroad for as long as these people retain their permanent place of residence in Romania. And it seems that the country can hardly afford the sums involved for those who are actually covered by state health insurance, let alone those outside the system.

No doubt there were initial complications, misunderstandings and cases of misuse by both states and individuals when the EHIC was first introduced. For example, in 2013 the European Commission was forced to take legal action against the Spanish government. It was reported that foreign tourists from the EU in need of emergency health care were made to pay for medical assistance in "hundreds of cases" regardless of the rules applying to EHIC holders. And yet private hospitals are exempt from having to provide treatment to such patients. There were similar cases in some of Austria's ski resorts and in Mediterranean countries at first— perhaps only because the project was new and unfamiliar. Or is the solidarity on which the EHIC is based limited to the members of their own community? Can that solidarity stand the test of a real crisis? These first experiences, made at the introduction of the universal "magic card," brought up the question, at least. And more doubts were to follow.

Questions soon arose about EHIC misuse among patients. Before the United Kingdom left the EU, the British media caused some panic by claiming that foreigners could easily obtain the card and use it to take advantage of the National Health Service (NHS), which was an abuse of taxpayers' money. (This scandal was very similar to the "Polish plumber" syndrome in France—a previously established stereotype that embodied the fear of the French that Poles were entering the country to steal their jobs.) In 2018 the tabloid *The Sun* published an alarming report under the headline EUROPEAN HEALTH TOURISM SCAM RIPPING NHS OFF BY £200 MILLION STILL GOING EIGHT MONTHS AFTER OUR EXPOSÉ. The newspaper had previously obtained thirteen fake EHIC cards, one in the name of a government minister, another in the name of U.S. president Donald Trump, in order to prove that the British NHS was easily abused.

Without going too much into the details of the *Sun* article, it was never really established how much of this alleged £200 million was actually linked to fake cards, nor how the reporters arrived at the strange number of 57 million cards—no less than a quarter of all cards issued in the EU. The suspicion that masses of Eastern Europeans were acquiring fake cards in the United Kingdom and sending them home to family members who for some reason did not have any health insurance at all was never proven.

It seems to me that the EHIC system depends on how serious the issuing country is about verifying where you pay your taxes, your country of residence and any health insurance contributions you make. On the other hand, hospitals abroad should also verify the identity of a patient presenting an EHIC.

All this panic over misuse is an overreaction to the excellent practice that is saving people's lives and making mobility within the EU, whether for work or tourism, easier and safer. The fear of misuse and fraud is a legitimate one, but if it is prompted by speculation alone rather than facts, then it could be harmful and prevent citizens from exercising rights to which they are entitled. According to data gathered by Eurostat in 2018, some 25 percent of EU citizens benefit from this card and most probably they feel the same sense of comfort as I do. If you ever wonder what Europeans hold in common—this is a Europe that most of us can identify with. But is this the last cry in favor of the former welfare states, or perhaps the beginning of it?

The real problems that Europeans should worry about are not fake health insurance cards, but bigger and bigger cuts in public expenditure, the privatization of health care, especially in Eastern European countries, and the consequent restrictions on public health care all over the EU. After the economic crisis of 2008, the largest cuts occurred in Greece, Ireland, Latvia and Portugal. But even rich countries like Sweden are raising the fee that patients must pay to visit a doctor and receive medicine. Everywhere, waiting lists for expensive MRI scans, diagnostic tests and surgery are growing longer and longer. All this ultimately means placing higher financial burdens on patients. The state, which once carried the main responsibility for providing health care for all, is gradually withdrawing under the pressure of the free market economy.

This situation is aggravated by the collapse of social solidarity and the kind of collective identification necessary to sustain the welfare state. Once a basic European value, solidarity is also threatened by the growing diversity of communities, something that has been accelerated by the recent mass influx of non-European immigrants. When push comes to shove, it seems that family, community and nation come before foreigners.

When the coronavirus hit Europe in the spring of 2020, the reaction to the pandemic delivered another proof of this nativist inclination. Not only did COVID-19 present a threat to people's health, it turned the previous EU health policy on its head. One of the first victims of the virus was free movement. Borders were closed, one after the other, and countries quickly started to turn inward. None of the cooperative pandemic strategies previously agreed on by the EU countries were implemented. Instead it was everyone for himself.

Italy quickly developed into Europe's coronavirus number-one hot spot and the pictures of overcrowded hospitals and long rows of coffins caused panic in neighboring countries. At the beginning, none of the fellow EU states were willing to help, concentrating instead on taking care of their own. Several countries—for example, Germany, France and the Czech Republic—even issued export bans on medical equipment, including protective gear such as masks and gloves, equipment that was badly needed in Bergamo or Bologna. European solidarity was nowhere to be seen.

At the end of March, parts of France were almost as badly hit as northern Italy had been a few weeks earlier; in these areas, hospitals were overrun by COVID-19 patients. In Alsace, a region bordering Germany, older patients were no longer put on ventilators but received only palliative care. Instead of trying to save these patients' lives, overwhelmed medical staff "treated" them with opiates and sleeping pills. Before the pandemic it was not uncommon for Alsatians to turn to German hospitals for treatment, since these facilities were sometimes closer than any in France. But not now. Now the border was closed and German hospitals were reserved for German residents.

The coronavirus triggered a radical renationalization that would have seemed unimaginable before the outbreak. Part of this was a kind of health isolationism that put everything the EHIC stands for into question. Is there a way back from there? The transnational public health reform that this card represents might be profound in its consequences, but is it anything more than a fair-weather friend?

After a while, the blatant lack of cooperation and solidarity among EU member states became too painful to bear, both politically and ethically. German hospitals finally opened up to not only French COVID-19 patients who needed to be put on ventilators, but also to some of the most severe cases from Italy. And so did the neighboring countries of Austria, Switzerland and Luxembourg. Late but still. And even though the help coordinated by the EU to the countries worst hit by the virus was slow to arrive, it exceeded by far the more media-effective goodwill actions by Russia and China.

According to a survey by the European Council on Foreign Relations, presented in June 2020, most Europeans were deeply disillusioned by the EU response to the coronavirus pandemic. Many—in France up to 58 percent—said that the EU was irrelevant during the first months of the crisis. At the same time, however, they expressed the desire for more cooperation in the future.

Already before the coronavirus crisis, it was clear that, in connection with EHIC, two parallel but contrasting processes are taking place in the EU. While on the one hand more and more people are becoming aware of the benefits it could bring, the historical achievements of the welfare state that are fundamental to this kind of health care are being dismantled. You cannot but wonder about the future of the EHIC. Is its golden age already behind us, even before all citizens have had the chance to experience its benefits? The future of the "magic card," the sign of a true European community, will not be any different than that of the European Union itself. I see it as a glue necessary to hold the whole thing together—a superglue that is as strong, perhaps, as the law against double tax-ation or the opportunity to buy property abroad. Why? Because it is proof of the welfare state, a state—or the union of states—that cares about its citizens as individuals. Insisting on the welfare com-ponent in leading a common life might indeed be the winning ar-gument for a lasting EU; it could help create the essential collective emotional identification that is currently missing.

Of course, we would need more superglues to connect us in or-der for this enlarged community to survive. One thing is sure, however: those of us who have needed to use such a card will try to do whatever we can for it—and for what is behind it—to stay alive.

Lost in Transition

*The long path from social
to private property*

When my mother died, I inherited some land on the island of Krk, Croatia, where her family came from. But instead of receiving the ownership document, I was only given a list of plots, seven of them. Or rather parts of plots, because in some instances a third, a fifth or even 20 out of 240 parts of a given plot were to be shared with a number of distant relatives. I had not even met most of them. Good news? No, not really. These plots are small, some are overgrown with the macchia bushes that are typical of the Mediterranean and others with neglected olive trees, some are pastures for sheep to graze on. And none of the plots is near the sea. None is in a building area. This means that their value would be low, should anyone want to buy such a plot at all.

Even if I did have a buyer for my small share, I could sell it only with the agreement of all the owners—provided that I first obtained a document certifying ownership in my name. This was to prove easier said than done. One would have thought that private property is sacrosanct, but it is not necessarily so, not in what is a former communist country.

The pieces of land I inherited are not even in my mother's name, but in the name of her father or aunt or someone else she inherited them from. In earlier times, people did not necessarily register the transfer of property, probably because of administrative costs and taxation. And like in every feudal country, as land was inherited, it was divided into smaller and smaller patches. As indicated in my mother's will, the first step in a long process of obtaining ownership documents was to transfer these "confetti" plots to my name. This is, as I gradually realized with each year that passed since her death, a long and painstaking procedure. But I felt obliged to do it out of respect for my mother and her long-gone relatives, who once scraped the money together to buy that land, worked on it and even earned their living from it in some cases.

Croatia inherited its land administration system from two states, the Austro-Hungarian Empire, which ruled the territory from 1527 to 1918, and the Socialist Federal Republic of Yugoslavia, which ruled from 1945 to 1991 (there was a short-lived kingdom in the intervening years). Then as now, land ownership was registered using two sets of documents, a cadastre and a land register, which should be regularly updated so that they correspond with each other. A cadastre contains maps of land plots with evidence of their extent and location as well as descriptions of cultivation practices and the buildings on each plot. But this alone is not a reliable source of ownership because of an old rule that not only the owner but also the leaseholder could register their ownership in the cadastre. Therefore, the only valid document of ownership is that from the land register. These two sources are complementary and should contain the same data. However, if ownership was not updated every time the plot changed hands, the documents will carry different data and confusion rules.

It took me some time just to understand how the system works.

This is where the European Union comes into my life and my attempt to get proper possession of my inheritance. One of the conditions of EU accession for each Eastern European country was to sort out property documentation and update and digitalize the two registers. Croatia is no exception when it comes to the property issue and, like the other countries affected, it received proceeds from the so-called accession funds to complete the task. The deadline for doing so was January 1, 2013, Croatia's year of accession to the EU.

With funds pouring in, the local administration on the island of Krk suddenly woke up from a long, undisturbed sleep and became very active. My mother got a formal letter from the mayor of her hometown, informing her that the municipality was preparing changes in accordance with the new EU rules. Every landowner had to visibly mark the borders of their land with cornerstones painted white. There were two ways of doing this: the more expensive one was to leave the task to the municipality to do for a fee. The cheaper way was to paint and lay out the cornerstones yourself. A contract came with the letter to the effect that if one chose to do the job oneself, the municipality would send the ownership documents once new records had been created using aerial photography, all the measurements had been taken and the two registers had been updated. Not trusting the municipality, my mother hired a man to mark her land; she even went with him to show him where her parcels were, and soon her part of the contract was fulfilled. At least, she remembered where these plots are, which I can't say I do. I have never visited them and would not have been able to find a single one.

Years passed and she did not hear from the Krk municipality. Not even after 2013, the year of accession, when Croatia became the twenty-eighth EU member state. It seems to me that, once in the EU, many projects slowed down or were just abandoned. I am not surprised: there are 3500 cadastre municipalities, 70 percent of which were last updated in the nineteenth century and 220 of which have no registers at all.

From time to time, my mother would call about the documents promised to her. If anyone picked up the phone (after it had rung for some considerable time), she would be informed that the deadline for updating the documents had been prolonged. And then prolonged again. Annoyed, she would hang up. Some eight years after starting the ownership procedure, my mother died, without ever having received any information about the state of her documents, never mind the documents themselves. Her long life and the experience she had accrued under four states and various political systems without ever moving from the place where she was born and where she would die—the Kingdom of Yugoslavia, the fascist Independent State of Croatia, the Socialist Federal Republic of Yugoslavia, the democratic Republic of Croatia—had taught her to collect each and every document available. I found them neatly sorted in an envelope bearing my name, a heap of old papers, some yellowish and worn at the edges, some of them handwritten with different stamps and seals and letterheads. With this envelope in hand, it was now my turn to follow up on her inquiries.

About a year after she passed away, the first letter from the cadastre in Krk arrived, still addressed to her. The letter was a call to attend the land registry office at the municipal court and present documents in order to personally confirm her ownership of the property. One step toward updating the cadastre, I thought. But I was angry because my mother could hardly "personally confirm" anything any longer. Moreover, I had been careful to inform all the relevant authorities about her passing away, so I called the number on the letter. We did not receive her death certificate from the municipality, a clerk explained; you would need to provide us with it, together with a copy of her will. No, it is not enough to send documents—you have to attend personally or send a lawyer, she said. "Is it the same procedure for each parcel of land?" I asked. The court clerk confirmed that it was. Moreover, the procedure would be repeated until every proprietor listed has finally attended; until that happens, the court cannot issue any ownership documents. And what about the contract with the municipality? Will the documents be sent to the owners for free? Yes. But the municipality will send out documents only once the court has finished updating the registers, explained the clerk. Then I, like my mother before me, hung up in despair. I felt dizzy. What had already seemed complicated enough was now even more so.

Time passed and I have been trying to get hold of my own property for five years now. Finally, I engaged a lawyer and we are still waiting for the court summonses for one parcel after the other. The EU deadline must have been prolonged again, since local administrations are obviously incapable of sorting out property issues within a given time frame. One thing has to be said, however: by 2016, all the documents had been made available online, a huge step forward in terms of accessing the files, but not much of an improvement when it comes to the painstaking process of establishing one's ownership.

Having documents correspond with one another is not only a problem in a small municipality like my mother's, which perhaps cannot be expected to have the resources for such a job. Zagreb, the capital of Croatia, has exactly the same problem. There too, the updating process is a sort of work in progress. Some years ago, I learned to my amazement that my apartment is located in a former garden. Long ago, the land on which it is built was once a big park with a fish pond where fat carps were bred for the Catholic priests living nearby. The park later shrank and part of it became someone's garden. The apartment building was completed in the early 1960s. It was a so-called socially owned property and was never properly registered in either set of records. So yes, apparently, I live on the third floor of a garden according to the cadastral map—while in the land register it is an apartment building. But at least I am the only owner and updating those records should be simpler.

In 1992, a way of bridging the gap between social and private ownership was introduced in the form of the "book of deposited contracts." Given that Croatia had been one of the six republics of the communist former Yugoslavia, there were two kinds of ownership by the 1990s, when private ownership of socially owned (*društveno vlasništvo*) apartment buildings became possible. Under the previous system, you would have to join a waiting list to get such an apartment in the first place. After waiting a long time, sometimes a decade or more, social apartments were allocated according to the number of merit points earned. The criteria included your seniority and the type of position you held at work, your age, your education and many other considerations—but Communist Party membership used to be decisive.

Without investing any of your own money, you could get tenant rights for life in these apartments. Your children could even inherit your rights. Although the flat belonged to the government, an enterprise or a political organization, tenants did have de facto property rights. When communism collapsed, the era of privatizing the social ownership of enterprises and real estate followed. Tenants in apartments with tenant rights were given the option (and cheap bank loans) to buy the apartment in which they lived for much less than the market price. Once all the ownership documents were properly updated so that they corresponded and were then filed, the contracts relating to the tenant's purchase of the apartment would be registered in the book of deposited contracts. This had the same legal status as the land register, but was meant to be an interim measure to ease property ownership issues arising from the two different kinds of ownership.

Buying such an apartment was not the end of the story. The properties incorporated common spaces like staircases, cellars, attics, laundry rooms, hallways and yards, ownership of which was also to be divided equally among tenants. The dividing up (*etažiranje*) of the properties also had to be recorded in the updated register and be done by a specialist agency according to law. The apartment house where I live was successfully divided before I moved in and has a common yard. Although it is not big—perhaps 500 square meters—because of the lack of parking space in central Zagreb, this yard became a much-sought-after space in which every apartment owner would like to be able park his or her car for free. However, the yard is not big enough for that. Furthermore, there are five makeshift tin garages in the middle of the yard, which were built in the communist days, all without permission. As a new owner, I came up with a brilliant idea: if all the apartment

owners agreed, we could take down the garages, reimburse owners and then allow some fifteen cars to park in the yard. I wondered
why nobody had suggested this idea before, but it soon became
apparent that such an agreement would be impossible for several
reasons: First of all, the yard belongs to the tenants of all three
buildings surrounding it and not only to those in our building.
And second, the yard cannot be divided between all the tenants
because the five garages were built before 1963, the year in which
the current legal property boundaries were established. So the
garages could not be demolished without extensive legal complications.

The same issues arise when communal spaces like staircases or
entrance halls need renovation or painting. There is a maintenance
fund into which we pay our dues each month, but it is too small for
major repairs. Our north-facing façade had started to crumble—
after all, the building is over fifty years old. As a result, the rooms
on the two top floors on that side of the building grow damp during
the winter. In order to have the necessary maintenance work done,
we the owners of the house need a bank loan cosigned by all ten of
us. But the owners on the lower floors initially refused to sign. It
took time to persuade them of the urgency of the matter, because
some found it hard to comprehend that we all jointly owned the
façade too.

This made me think that to own property in such a country is
not as great as it may sound.

This problem of commonly owned space became even more obvious during a visit to Bulgaria. My friend has a nice small flat in
an apartment building in Sofia that was socially owned under communism. When I visited her in 2003, I was surprised to find the
entrance hall, the staircase and the elevator in a rather abominable

state. There were broken bulbs, the paint was peeling off the walls and the door at the main entrance was half broken down. But when I entered her apartment and that of her neighbor, I was startled by their elegant and tasteful interiors. By that time all former tenants had bought their apartments and taken great care to refurbish them in style. But the care and investment ended at their apartment doors. Once outside the private sphere, you entered a no-man's-land just like in the entrance hall. Then my friend took me to a newly built area on the outskirts of Sofia, where the amazing villas of the nouveaux riches were surrounded by high walls equipped with security cameras. Expensive cars were parked in front of the villas. The affluence of these house owners was manifest, and I almost felt as if I was visiting a gated community somewhere in the rich West.

There was only one difference. The day before our sightseeing tour, it rained heavily and we found ourselves walking through mud. There were no asphalt roads, only dirt paths between the houses, each house worth a fortune. Road building and maintenance are the responsibility of the municipality, which evidently lacks resources. The beautiful villas were actually planted in the mud. Why had the owners not invested in asphalt roads? Well, that is another question. Or perhaps not, as I did see such privately financed "improvements" in a public space in downtown Sofia. There, in front of the fancy shops and boutiques, you could often see a dilapidated pavement patched up with a few square meters of asphalt, sometimes even cobblestones or bricks. Potholes in front of Max Mara or Dior would not look good. Moreover, they could be dangerous, especially as women in Sofia love to wear very high heels, I noticed.

When it comes to dealing with private property, there are always more unpleasant surprises in store than one expects. For example, in the former Yugoslavia we had entire neighborhoods consisting of houses built without permission or any regard for city planning at all. This so-called black housing was situated on the outskirts of cities and especially along the Adriatic coast. Such family homes were usually self-built concrete nightmares but ostensibly tolerated by the authorities because of the general lack of housing (the likelihood of bribes paid by owners could not be excluded, however). The post-communist government did not quite know how to handle this illegal housing issue. At one point they started a demolition campaign, but they soon realized that it would be more useful to legalize the buildings. As a result, if you wish to buy a house today, especially on the coast, there is more to worry about than just land registry issues. You also have to check whether the house was legalized within the prescribed deadline. If it was not, there is no longer any possibility of entering any kind of legalization process. Such a house will most probably end up being demolished. But even that is not certain, because the law could change again.

Depending on the region in which you want to buy a house, there may yet be additional things to worry about. If the house is located in a former war zone or a region of ethnic cleansing, then psychological and moral issues must be taken into account as well as administrative ones. Last year, my daughter decided to buy a summer house and was about to take a look at one on offer. Only a half-hour drive from Zagreb, the modest house was situated in an orchard near a small river and seemed like an ideal weekend retreat. I was not immediately conscious of my doubts about this property, but I had an uneasy feeling about its location close to the town of Karlovac. In 1991–92, this property was in a war zone. Could it have formerly belonged to Serbs who were forced to flee

Croatia? Was it nationalized afterward, then returned to the owner selling it now, years later, having lost the desire to pick fruit in a place he was once chased out of, perhaps by his own neighbors? Or was the house purchased by somebody who got hold of the documents illegally?

Such cases had occurred before. I know a man who made his living buying the houses of Serbian refugees: he would buy them cheaply and sell them for a profit a couple of years later, when the prices went up. Profiting from the misfortune of others did not bother him much. Whether my daughter's choice of property was just such a case, I don't know, but I can say that I was relieved when she gave up on it.

My own experience of private property and that of people I know leads me to understand that both "private" and "property" are vague and very relative categories in my part of Europe. There are many reasons for this, ranging from political and economic changes through social ownership and war to ethnic cleansing and the Holocaust.

Watching the Hungarian movie *1945*, directed by Ferenc Török and released in 2017, is perhaps the best way to understand at least one aspect of this; good films sometimes make such things possible. It begins with two strangers, Orthodox Jews, disembarking from a train at a small railway station in the middle of nowhere. They have two big boxes with them, almost like coffins. The railway station worker takes his bicycle and departs for the village in a great hurry to deliver news of their arrival. Meanwhile, villagers prepare for the wedding of a son of a local businessman who took over the local shop after the Jewish owners were transported to a concentration camp. As the two new arrivals approach the village on foot, the news spreads and people panic. They are afraid that the two Jews are coming back to reclaim the property of their relatives, who had been deported a year or two before. In the meantime everything has been stolen by the villagers—the shop, the tavern, the houses. Why are these two returning? And what is in their big boxes? Maybe the goods they want to sell once they have taken back the shop? Everybody took part in the plundering, so everybody has reason to fear the two strangers approaching. . . .

This black-and-white movie, in a style close to that of a documentary, shows the collective fear of the return of rightful owners, and how it destroys a community built on lies, denunciations and theft.

But this happened all over Eastern Europe and not only to Jews. Some three million ethnic Germans were expelled or had to flee their homes during the aftermath of World War II from the part of Czechoslovakia annexed by Hitler in 1938. Of course, local people promptly moved into those vacated houses. When thirty years later, two strangers suddenly appeared in a local tavern in a small village there, they were met with an awkward silence and suspicion. Perhaps these two men came because they wanted their family's property back? But they were only two journalists in search of a good story, who, as it happens, got a unique chance to experience firsthand the mistrust of those living in and from stolen property.

When do wars really end? It seems that wars continue to live on in property documents, in doubts, nightmares and fears for generations.

The Hungarian movie reminded me of my own experience of an abandoned village in Istria. Istria is a peninsula now in Croatia and previously part of Italy and Austria. Various feudal lords have fought over the territory for centuries. The last significant wave of migration took place there after World War II. This region was incorporated into Yugoslavia after Tito arrived with his army in Trieste, an important port on the Adriatic Sea that the Allies wanted Italy to keep.

In exchange for withdrawing its army from Trieste, Yugoslavia received a peninsula that was divided into zones A and B, controlled by the Allies and Tito's army, respectively. As soon as this news reached Istria, masses of people started an exodus toward Italy. Many were afraid to be proclaimed Fascist collaborators, others belonged to the Italian minority that Benito Mussolini, the Italian Fascist dictator, had settled in Istria, and still others did not like the idea of living under a communist regime. People were in such a hurry to leave that they left behind animals in their stables, food cooking on the stove, a table laid for lunch. In the spring of 1945, a Croatian acquaintance arrived with his partisan detachment in the little town of Motovun, only to find it totally abandoned but for a dead-drunk Italian pharmacist, who must have started drinking from his stocks early that morning.

The exodus had started after the capitulation of Italy in 1943. An even greater number left during the period from 1945 to 1947—as many as 100,000, depending on the source. In 1947, however, Istrian Italians were given the chance to opt for Italy. Once again, villages were deserted overnight and soon enough those who stayed plundered the houses of those who had fled. But many houses remained abandoned for as long as they had a good roof. As soon as water came through the roof, the walls made out of soft limestone and mud would collapse. Even today there are many ruins and dilapidated houses there. The communist government that nationalized or confiscated them after the war promised to take care of those properties, but that never happened.

I once entered such a ghost house during a walk with a friend.

She had purchased a small, renovated house in a medieval town near Motovun and wanted to show me the surroundings. We entered because there were no doors; they had probably been removed to be installed in a nearby house. The few things left behind were dirty and neglected. The kitchen table with a few chairs around it was laid with a now tattered tablecloth; there was a kitchen cupboard with a few broken glasses and cups and a blackened wood oven that no longer functioned. One window had no pane and only the sad-looking rags of what once must have been white curtains with a pattern of small red flowers. I am sure that older people in the nearby villages knew to whom the house belonged and who plundered it as well, just like in the Hungarian film.

Under the Osimo Agreement of 1975 and the Rome Agreement of 1983, exiles were granted compensation. My friend bought her house in 1989, just before Yugoslavia fell apart. Soon, the house found itself in the new, post-communist state. The Republic of Croatia started to restitute nationalized and confiscated property to its previous owners only after 1997, so many claims of ownership remained unresolved for the time being. This was the case with the small fenced parcel of land of about forty square meters right in front of her house. The little plot belonged to different owners—to the state, the municipality (thanks to nationalization) and an unknown private owner who was either abroad or dead, or perhaps unaware of his inheritance. Carlo, one of her neighbors, used to walk around the village drunk, pointing at houses and gardens, saying this is mine, this too, and this. . . . It seemed as if he owned half the place, whereas in fact he probably owned about a twentieth or a fiftieth—or just a "confetti" piece!—of each property.

In other words, because of the legal transition from social to private property, and the contested legacies of nationalization and restitution, the plot in front of her house could be partly rented out and was partly unavailable. As it was so small and directly in front of her door, she used it like a garden without giving much thought to renting it out; buying it was impossible for the time being. Her problem arose when she thought she should buy it just so that the yard she had been using for twenty years as her own actually became hers. In the meantime this had become legally possible. The way to buy it was via public tender. My friend was quite surprised to discover that she was not alone in trying to buy the small plot before her door. A neighbor across the street had also put in a bid, although for seemingly obscure reasons because she did not or could not use it, or fence it in. What could she possibly do beyond placing a flowerpot or two there? But the neighbor managed to buy one part, while my friend bought another.

She learned that the parts of the plot that were social property could be claimed as the property of the long-term user (*dosjelost*). However, such cases had to be decided in court. So my friend took the case to court—but lost. Today, five years later, there are still several owners of that forty-square-meter patch outside her door: herself, the neighbor across the street, the state, the municipality and the unknown owner, each possessing a portion of the plot. This means that it is not possible to draw boundaries, so none of them knows which part belongs to whom. With the benefit of hindsight, it seems clear that the neighbor did not want her tiny plot either for growing flowers or sunbathing there, but to cause the value of my friend's house to drop, should she wish to sell it. In other words, if my friend wanted to avoid her property's falling in value, she would have to buy her neighbor out for a much higher price than the neighbor could have otherwise hoped for.

If all this sounds like a nightmare, it is because private property is still lost in transition in many countries in Eastern Europe. How to buy and sell property if no one can be sure of what belongs to whom in the first place? If laws exist but are not respected or applied because of red tape or corruption—or, more likely, a combination of the two? Hopefully, one day this will all be sorted out and data will be transcribed into the land registry and cadastres updated in all former communist countries. Until that day one cannot be sure whether people like Carlo are right when they point to their ownership of every second plot of land, but they can continue to do so as long as ownership has yet to be established and properly recorded.

In Croatia that day does not look like it is going to come any time soon. However, in September 2018 Croatia's Ministry of Finance and the World Bank signed project financing to the tune of €19.7 million for an integrated land administration system. This was good, because this will fund improvements to the system, although the money has to be paid back of course. Nevertheless, the work is far from finished. That said, as in other former communist countries, money seems to have its own mysterious ways of disappearing.

The Holocaust
and Memory Theft

*On different ways to
commemorate*

One night in December 2018, a strange hole was dug in the pavement of a street in the center of Rome. On Via Madonna del Monti, twenty small square brass-plated plaques were removed from in front of house no. 81. A shallow asphalt pit remained in their stead. The stolen plaques are not just any plaques, but "stumbling stones," *stolpersteine*—special monuments to deported and murdered Jews and other victims of the Holocaust. While their material value is negligible, they are valuable because they indicate the full name, year of birth, and date of deportation and death of each Jewish person who once lived in this building. That is, all eighteen members of the Di Consiglio family and two from the Di Castro family. Most of them were deported to Auschwitz in 1944 and died either there or in an unknown place.

There was a public outcry in Italy and elsewhere in response to this act of vandalism, which was instantly recognized as anti-Semitism. Politicians were quick to express their outrage, including

Matteo Salvini, the right-wing minister of the interior. They promised to swiftly find the culprits, as they always do, though this is of little consolation. Regardless of who did it, the theft remains one of many signs of a reviving anti-Semitism, part of the wave of xenophobia that surfaced with mass immigration from the Middle East and Africa in 2015. If anti-Semitism seems like a kind of by-product or something that is happening on the margins of the rise of the political right in Europe, this impression is wrong. Were it to occur anywhere other than Europe, one could dismiss it as ephemeral. But in Europe, acts of anti-Semitism cannot be marginal. On the contrary, we know this because such acts have happened before. Anti-Semitism in Europe is part and parcel of the anti-immigration movement because Jews are perceived as eternal Others, eternal immigrants, strangers, those who do not belong and who could never be assimilated. The revival of anti-Semitism today is a yardstick for measuring other expressions of xenophobia and hatred. In the territory where six million Jews were murdered, many of them made literarily to vanish into thin air, anti-Semitism is the alarm bell for how far frustrations with Others—now immigrants—have already advanced. Not only in Italy, but in Germany and Poland, in Hungary and in France—where, for example, eighty-five-year-old Mireille Knoll was stabbed and burned to death in her Paris flat in March 2018. Her murder is the latest in a series, following the shootings of a teacher and three children from a Jewish school in Toulouse in 2012 and of four people in a kosher supermarket in Paris in 2015. In November 2018, the French government announced a 69 percent increase in anti-Semitic acts during the first nine months of the year. This is referred to as the "new anti-Semitism" and blamed on "Islamic radicalization."

"It's an anti-Semitism of ignorance, poverty and the ghetto,"

Karim Amellal, a French Algerian academic, told National Public Radio. "And it just so happens that most of the people living in these kinds of neighborhoods are Muslims."

In Hungary, Prime Minister Viktor Orbán repeatedly accused the Jewish entrepreneur, millionaire and philanthropist George Soros of a conspiracy to bring immigrants to Europe to destroy the European way of life. In Poland, beyond everyday manifestations of anti-Semitism in the press, in graffiti, on social media, etc., the conservative Law and Justice Party passed a law that makes the use of expressions like "Polish concentration camp" a punishable offense because, it is argued, responsibility for the crimes that took place on Polish soil lay elsewhere. This law makes it illegal to say that the Polish state or the Polish nation participated in the Holocaust, despite the estimates of experts that between 62,000 and 200,000 Jewish people were either killed or reported by Poles during World War II. After the law was passed, acts of anti-Semitism increased.

In Germany, the right-wing, racist and anti-Semitic Alternative for Germany (AfD) was elected to the Bundestag for the first time in 2017. Elsewhere, ultra-nationalist parties already in power or very much part of mainstream politics, such as the Freedom Party of Austria, Golden Dawn in Greece, Jobbik in Hungary or the Sweden Democrats, are openly anti-Semitic or have a fascist past.

That there is reason for concern was confirmed in November 2018, when CNN published the results of an opinion poll in which more than seven thousand people were interviewed, with respondents distributed equally among Austria, France, Germany, the United Kingdom, Hungary, Poland and Sweden. According to this poll, one in twenty Europeans has never heard of the Holocaust. The situation is the worst in France, where one in five aged between eighteen and thirty-four has never heard of the Holocaust. Even in Austria, the homeland of Hitler, 12 percent of youngsters have never heard of the Holocaust. There is a tight connection between attitudes to Israel and feelings of anti-Semitism: more than a quarter of respondents said that anti-Semitism was a response to actions taken by the state of Israel. When it comes to the proportion of the world's population that is Jewish, estimates exceeded the real figure of 0.2 percent by as much as a factor of 100. This poll also throws light on attitudes toward other minorities: 36 percent of Europeans said they view immigrants unfavorably.

Memory forms the essence of both individual and collective identity. The pit in Rome in front of house no. 81 represents a theft of the memory of the Holocaust. Digging out and removing small square plaques is therefore a highly symbolic act, as well as a warning sign: Watch out, here we come again to get you. First we steal your plaques and destroy material memory. Then we shut up people who still remember, then we come after everyone we don't like.

The brass plaques are easy to replace—but how can the loss of memory be prevented? Justice for the victims is secured only when the truth can no longer be denied. Removing their names is denial.

If indeed a third of Europeans polled said they knew only very little or nothing at all about the Holocaust, one must ask: How is it possible not to know or only to "know very little"? There are victims who are still alive and numerous museums and monuments commemorating the Holocaust all over Europe. If it is not about forgetting—for how can young people forget something they don't know?—perhaps it has to do with the ways of commemorating.

Remembrance depends first and foremost on education programs and history textbooks, but also on familial upbringing, social environment and culture, all of which does or perhaps does not facilitate remembrance. Visual reminders, like stumbling stones, monuments, sculptures, museums, memorial buildings and so on, serve the same purposes when it comes to information and education. Even more so because visual reminders are highly symbolic. We still remember the fall of the statue of Saddam Hussein in 2003 or the toppled statues of Stalin and Lenin all over the former communist world after 1989. But the creation of such sculptures and monuments rarely comes into public focus, except perhaps post facto. There are architects and artists who specialize in monuments—though such questions, in the end, concern everybody.

German artist Gunter Demnig probably had this in mind in 1992, when he started the project to place stumbling stones throughout Europe, wherever victims of the Holocaust had lived or been deported from. Since then, they have been placed in about a thousand cities, including for other victims of the Nazi regime such as homosexuals, communists and Jehovah's Witnesses. Demnig's idea of commemorating victims by writing down their names is not new—many monuments consist of a list of names engraved in memorial walls, sculptures, etc. But Demnig adds another dimension to the process by placing individual names on plaques in the pavement, marking the very place from where they were taken away never to return, so that people "stumble" on them, notice them, grow curious, become disturbed, are reminded, remember. The thieves in Rome surely knew this. It is therefore worth taking a look at such mementos, at these 10-centimeter-square plates with names and further information. But it is also worth considering them in relation to other monuments commemorating the Holocaust and victims of genocide, because there are different ways of keeping memory alive.

One literally stumbles repeatedly upon such metal tiles with commemorative inscriptions when walking the streets of Berlin.

There are so many that it is hard not to notice them. I stumbled upon a few near the Hackesche Höfe complex of beautiful art deco buildings and inner courtyards in what was once East Berlin. They are kept clean and shiny; the names and years are easy to read. At first, I thought I would need to ask someone what these small shiny things fixed in the sidewalk are and why there are so many. But as I paused and read the inscriptions, no additional explanation was needed. The magic of stumbling stones worked immediately: as soon as I read the names and the years of birth and death, I started to imagine people, their fear and their despair.

I remember lifting my gaze from four of the stumbling stones toward the façade of the house from where the whole Schneebaum family was deported to Auschwitz and *ermordet*, murdered: Hermann who at the time was thirty-eight years old, his thirty-three-year-old wife, Jenny, and their children, Thea, age twelve, and Victor, who was only two. I noticed an open window on the second floor. Of course, I didn't know why I had chosen that particular window, perhaps because of a white curtain that was fluttering as if trying to fly away. I couldn't help but imagine the moment Jenny was forced to leave the apartment with Victor in her arms. What did she wear?—the question appears out of nowhere, or perhaps not, because it was late autumn when I stood in front of that house—did she take her coat? Good shoes? Or grab whichever clothes lay at hand, since she did not know in all probability where she was going. But she knew why—she knew well, she must have known, as by then she was forced to wear a yellow star. What else did she take with her? I wonder. Her boy's favorite toy? A book perhaps, just because this would have been my choice? Perhaps she was a practical person who took some valuables, clothes and food.... The point is that when you see the name and stand there wondering, Jenny, mother of two, becomes a real person, someone you can identify with. You start to imagine her life in a way that may or may not be true, because the only truth is inscribed on a stumbling stone: that she was born in 1908 and murdered in Auschwitz in 1943.

When I am in Vienna's Sixth District, I often pass Aegidigasse. In that short street of unassuming façades nothing catches your eye. There are no shop windows or historical buildings. But if you happen to walk on the same side of the street as a five-story white-grayish building and look at the sidewalk in front of no. 5, you would likely stumble—as you should. Or at least I presume so, though these metal tiles are not as clean as those in Berlin and the names on them are barely visible. If you look harder, you see monuments commemorating infamous acts. This house was one of the collection points where Viennese authorities summoned Jews for transport. It is very conveniently located only a few hundred meters from the railway station, the Westbahnhof, a ten-minute walk from where Jewish people would start their journey in cattle trains to concentration camps in Riga, Lodz or Kowno and executions in Minsk, in November and December of 1941. Alfred Steiner, Anna Heilinger, Sofie Fries and Schulem Hirschfeld were some of the sixty Jews taken away from that house. Suddenly you see in your mind's eye sleepy and cranky children, their mother wondering why nobody told them where they were going and for how long. In 1938 Vienna had a Jewish population of nearly 200,000. By the end of the war, 65,000 Jews had been murdered—this number is engraved on the base of the city's Holocaust Memorial.

Only a couple of minutes away from Aegidigasse there was another house where Jewish people were also summoned for deportation. It is a school now. A few years ago, thirty-two stumbling stones were built into the pavement in front of the entrance. But not for long. They were removed and mounted on the wall instead, perhaps because kids were playing on them and jumping over them, not paying any attention to the commemorative purpose of the plaques. There is an argument that the indifference of people to the plaques at their feet amounts to a second death for the victims. Maybe that argument prevailed in this case? This is the reason Munich is a city where no one can stumble, since there are no stumbling stones. The Jewish community in Munich opposed the project, arguing that "having people tread upon the names of the dead and allowing dogs to urinate on these plaques is no memorial at all, but an insult to their identities."

Even if the plaques were transferred to the wall out of respect, it is wrong to move them from the pavement to the wall. There they look more like a kind of boring decoration than something one should look at carefully. As when reading the names of a husband and wife, Ernst Susser and Paula Susser (née Kosalik), deported from here on November 28, 1941, to Minsk and thinking for a moment of these two people whose only solace must have been that they were together in that dreadful moment.

Plaques attached to the wall are meaningless. Anything could be written on them, such as a warning that spitting on the floor is prohibited, or that smoking is forbidden here—any kind of nonsense. It doesn't matter because nobody looks. For this kind of remembrance, it is essential to find the small square reminders in an everyday context, on the way to the supermarket or a bus stop or school. One can stumble only where one walks. You pass by a hundred times; children step up on them without paying any attention, without respect; most passersby ignore them and walk over them just like over a sewer lid, without stumbling. However, if the plaques are on the pavement instead of the wall, there is a chance that one day at least one person will stumble. Instead of stepping on them blindly, he or she will stop. Maybe because strong rainfall had washed the dirt off, the brass will shine again and that person will take a look and ask: What is this? At that moment, placing a stumbling stone on the sidewalk is justified.

We do not remember Jewish people and other victims of fascism and their destiny every day, but only occasionally, as when a crime is committed like in Rome. And perhaps we fully grasp the meaning of stumbling stones only when we start to notice their *absence* and ask ourselves: Why are they not here too? Why are there so few? Does nobody in this town remember the people's names, dates, where they were taken from? Or could it be that such mementos, such reminders, are omitted on purpose?

In my own country, Croatia, there are four stumbling stones dedicated to Jewish victims, all in the town of Rijeka. They were put there in 2013 for Eugenio Lipschitz and Giannetta Zipser Lipschitz, with inscriptions in Croatian and Italian—hence there are four of them. Both people were murdered in Auschwitz. Why such commemoration only in Rijeka? Does Zagreb, the capital, have some other kind of monuments commemorating victims of the Holocaust?

A plaque on the side façade of a parking lot in the very center of Zagreb says, "Here stood a synagogue destroyed by the authorities in 1941." If there was a synagogue, there must have been people worshipping there from among the Jewish community of 11,000. Where did these people live? Where are the buildings from which they were deported? Was it from one of the five-story buildings on Draskoviceva or Ilica streets? Walking there, you would not know this to be the case, because there are no stumbling stones to remind you, no telling little reminders that should have been placed in front of the many, many buildings from which Jewish people were deported to Jasenovac, the Croatian concentration and death camp nearby. The name Jasenovac is engraved on the base of the Holocaust Memorial in Vienna, together with the names of forty-five other camps. In Zagreb, the notable absence of any commemoration of the victims is chilling.

Croatia, as one of the six republics of the federal state of Yugoslavia, found itself on the winning side at the end of World War II. But from 1941 to 1945 it was an independent Nazi puppet state with its own concentration and death camps for communists, Serbs, Jews and Roma people. The best known and most infamous one was Jasenovac. More than 80,000 people perished there, most of them civilians. Among these people were some 20,000 Jews out of the 30,000 living in Croatia at that time. There is a list preserved with the names of over 13,000 of those Jewish victims.

The Zagreb city government has announced a plan to build a memorial to Holocaust victims in the near future. But there has already been a monument in the Jasenovac memorial complex since 1966, when a giant sculpture was completed by the exiled dissident Bogdan Bogdanović, an architect, sculptor, writer and the former mayor of Belgrade. His *Stone Flower* commemorates all the victims of the camp, including Jewish people. You see it from afar as you approach the small town of Jasenovac, a fine sculpture some thirty meters high, hovering over nearby fields with four petals reaching toward the sky. In the place where so many people met their death, Bogdanović wanted to plant a symbol of life. Life that is fragile but resistant, just like a flower, he said.

As impressive as the work is, it has a completely different effect on the visitor than the small reminders one stumbles upon in the streets. For all its importance and even beauty, it is hard to take in, to appropriate as the symbol of human suffering that it was intended to be. You can admire it, but perhaps admiration should not be the overwhelming feeling here.

However, something else got stuck in my mind ever since I visited the place a long time ago with my elementary school class. Jasenovac concentration camp was Croatian, not German. There were no gas chambers built there to facilitate mass killings. People were murdered by the hands of their executors, just like a sheep or a goat. I remember an exhibition of the different tools with which wardens used to do the job. Among them were different kinds of knives, axes, a big wooden hammer. And I remember looking at them and feeling nauseated. I had never seen an animal slaughtered, much less a human being. But standing there, I could imagine it. I never forgot these tools.

Many years later, in 1995, I visited Jasenovac again. But the memorial complex had all but disappeared. The windows and doors of the building were gone, and only broken glass vitrines and garbage remained. The exhibits had been looted. I suspect that this is the only vandalized Holocaust monument in Europe, all thanks to the fact that the territory had changed hands during the 1991–92 war, when it passed from Croatian to Serbian forces. It was almost unbearable to see the ruined museum and the visitor book full of pupils' handwriting, which seemed to have been thrown around and now lay there, half destroyed by the rain. Bogdanovic's flower still stood, untouched. He was happy about that, he said once.

The memorial center was later restored by the Croatian government, but this does not mean that the victims it commemorates were treated with respect. For example, in 2016, despite the proximity of the death camp, a plaque with the salute of the Ustashe, Croatian fascist soldiers during World War II, was attached to the façade of a house in the town of Jasenovac. This abominable act was not followed by the removal of the plaque and the arrest of the perpetrators. To the dismay of many citizens, it remained there for a year, while the government formed a commission to decide what to do. Then the government opted to mount it at the entrance of the town of Novska, some ten kilometers away and about twenty meters from a now destroyed antifascist monument to 650 fighters and civilians killed by the Ustashe in 1945. The reason why it still stands is because it commemorated Croatian soldiers fighting in the 1991 "Homeland War" and was put up by war veterans. The infamous salute was habitually used in that war, in which army units were named after Croatian war criminals from World War II. The police did not arrest people making this salute on different occasions and raising their hands to form a Croatian Sieg Heil— nor did these people end up in court.

On the other hand, there are no commemorative plaques at sites of concentration camps and mass executions other than Jasenovac. Any that existed previously have been destroyed. Croats do not want to remember the antifascist past because antifascism coincides with communism. More than three thousand antifascist monuments were destroyed in Croatia after the collapse of communism in a clear demonstration of contempt for the victims of fascism; many were the work of well-known sculptors.

This kind of tolerance of vandalism and fascist salutes by the authorities is only one sign of the galloping revision of history in Croatia. Revisionism is the reason stumbling stones for Holocaust victims are not likely to appear in Croatia.

The material destruction of antifascist monuments equals the hole in the pavement in Rome after the theft of stumbling stones; it is a prelude to the theft and rewriting of history. Today, pupils no longer read Anne Frank's diary in elementary school. In 2018 only fifteen school groups visited the Jasenovac memorial complex.

When I was a schoolchild in the early sixties, we were bused around on excursions to other important antifascist memorials relating to World War II—for example, one in Tjentište, on the river Sutjeska in Bosnia and Herzegovina, where a battle against the German army changed the course of the war in Yugoslavia. In raw nature surrounded by mountains, two huge stone blocks, like wings some twenty meters high, protrude from the earth as if a giant angel is trying to get out from underneath. It is frightening and makes human beings seem small and perishable—if that was the idea, then it works. To tell the truth, for us teenagers the battle was more memorable after seeing *The Battle of Sutjeska*, a 1973 film starring Richard Burton as Tito, who was commanding the Yugoslav partisan army.

The winners of World War II delivered a crash course in history by erecting not only social realist but also modernist monuments (Yugoslavia was an exception in this respect). I am sure that we listened to lectures in history right at the spot, next to monuments, a kind of history that bombards you with hard facts which you are expected to learn by heart. But it was hard to remember any such obligatory ritualization of the past, much less to feel pity for victims.

Monuments commemorating the Holocaust in Berlin and Vienna are no less abstract and difficult to interpret than those commemorating victims in Jasenovac or Tjentište. The famous Memorial to the Murdered Jews of Europe in Berlin, which opened in 2005 in Cora-Berliner-Strasse, dominates the scenery. The big field of concrete blocks, 2711 of them, each the approximate size of a coffin or grave, are arranged in orderly rows like in a graveyard. Although the architect, Peter Eisenman, has denied any association with a graveyard, it is actually not up to him to decide how visitors should experience the memorial. But perhaps he was right because these blocks, unlike tombstones, bear no names; they are anonymous. No feelings are possible, no sense of identification. If you happen to be there without knowing what it is, you would be at a loss. And you are at a loss anyway, because it is not immediately apparent why the Jews died (the word "Holocaust" is not mentioned in the title) or who they were—there are no individual names. The names are in a separate place, a room in the information center within the complex. Can monuments make us remember and forget victims at the same time? Yes, these coffins did just that for me: there were Jews living here—and then they were gone. We don't know who made them disappear or why. In any case, it is certain that the intended overall impression is one of solemnity. Yet even that is not guaranteed, as on a nice day tourists and visitors sit on the blocks and children climb on them and play hide-and-seek among them.

In the middle of one of the prettiest squares in the heart of Vienna's old town, there stands a huge cement block, as if it has been forgotten about after all the other buildings were completed. One wonders if that was the intention, to put the Holocaust Memorial there as a huge, all-too-huge, stone crypt, in order to purposefully obstruct the nice view, to remind us of those who suddenly were denied their lives here in Vienna, denied all sense of belonging, denied their humanity.

This cement square, 10 meters long by 7 meters wide and 3.8 meters high, reminds me, once again, of a huge tomb or bunker. But it is neither a tomb nor a bunker; the designer, Rachel Whiteread, envisioned the shelves of a library with books turned inside out. Therefore, it is also known as the Nameless Library, which supposedly suggests that Jews are the People of the Book. If you get closer you can see vertical elements that could represent books and of course some visitors see them, but not everyone does. The base on which the memorial stands has the names of forty-six concentration camps engraved on it, which should give the visitor an idea of what it commemorates. But if one hasn't already heard of these names—Auschwitz, Theresienstadt, Buchenwald, Dachau—this doesn't help.

One single detail evokes horror: there is a fake wooden door on one side, but this door has no handles. If you enter, there is no way out.

However, another monument in Vienna incited controversy. In 1991 a sculpture of a Jew forced to kneel and scrub the streets was erected on Albertinaplatz. This is one of many ways that Jews were humiliated after Hitler's Germany annexed Austria in 1938. But the sculpture by Alfred Hrdlicka did not necessarily prompt intended empathy. Many careless tourists used to sit on the back of the scrubbing man without necessarily being fully aware of what they were doing. In the end barbed wire was wrapped around it to prevent the monument's being used as a resting place—but dogs continue to pee on it.

These two ways of commemorating, stumbling stones and monuments, although they evoke different responses, are not mutually exclusive. On the contrary, they relate to each other like history and memory—their aim is the same, to prevent the loss of memory, but also to prevent the theft of memory. Is the mass killing of anonymous people easier to bear than the mass killing of people with names and stories, who are old and young, men and women, from this or that house, floor, apartment, room, bed? Perhaps this dilemma is best illustrated by the unique Anne Frank House memorial in Amsterdam. It is not only the apartment with its hidden part, but a reconstruction of the life in hiding led by Anne Frank and her family. That victim had a name and a life, and visiting the house containing the ordinary things she used brings her to life, makes her a person, one of us—just as her diary does. Even though this is a commemoration of a single life, it also commemorates all murdered Jews because, as a visitor, you have a chance to experience something of how she lived in hiding for more than two years, to see the tiny secret annex of 46 square meters, the complicated system of living there that was maintained by four family members and four other Jews. No wonder that over a million people visit it annually.

There are other ways to commemorate victims besides such visible symbols.

I learned this from the example of the latest mass killing in Europe. It happened in July 1995 in Srebrenica, Bosnia and Herzegovina, and was declared a genocide by the International Criminal Tribunal for the former Yugoslavia. The army of Republika Srpska, under the command of General Ratko Mladic, entered a zone protected by Dutch U.N. peacekeeping soldiers, separated men from women and shot more than 8000 men (mostly civilians) over the course of a couple of hot summer days. In Srebrenica, there are no stumbling stones but there is a Srebrenica Genocide Memorial with 6504 graves marked by *nišan*, white headstones that are characteristic for Muslims from Bosnia and Herzegovina. Those victims whose remains were found ended up at this graveyard, while many others still have yet to be found. The names of all those executed there are engraved on the marble wall within the complex.

I remember my own bewilderment and horror when the first reports of the massacre hit the news. Years later, during Slobodan Milošević's trial at the International Criminal Tribunal in The Hague in 2003, a survivor of the Srebrenica massacre testified. He was Protected Witness B-1401, a young man who, back then, when he stood before a firing squad, was only seventeen, said: "Some people begged them to give us water first and then kill us. I felt sad that I would die thirsty. When it was my turn, I went out and saw rows of corpses. I thought how my mother would never know where I was. . . ."

From Auschwitz to Srebrenica, the perpetrators don't expect anyone to survive. Survivors talk, testify, ask for justice and go on doing so for decades because war crimes never grow cold. Therefore, one way to remember Srebrenica or any such place is that we, the visitors, remember one sentence spoken by an eyewitness, or at least one name of a victim. I know that I will never forget the sentence "I felt sad that I would die thirsty," voiced by Witness B-1401. That sentence is my personal reminder.

In commemorating victims, we should remind ourselves that people are individuals, not a mass, even if counted in millions. To try to remember them as a mass in any form is to denigrate them, reduce them even further, to annihilate them again, just as their murderers would want. These murderers wanted them not to be people. Monuments should not contribute to that. Otherwise they become part of the culture of forgetting and denial.

We let ourselves forget simply because it is easier to forget, but to do so in a time of anxiety and fear is irresponsible: it is to grant ignorance free rule. After all, how and what we want to remember—or don't want to remember—tells us about ourselves, about who we are.

The United States
of Europe?

East European migration fever

It was around 1905 when my great-grandfather Petar Kraljić boarded a huge steamship in Fiume (or Rijeka in Croatian), then an Austro-Hungarian seaport in the northern Adriatic.

A few days before he boarded that steamship, my maternal great-grandmother stood on the pier of her home island's port dressed in her best with a white embroidered kerchief in her hand to dry her tears and wave as the local liner from their native island left for Fiume. She was to look after four small children on her own for the next five years, until her husband had earned the money to pay back the debt for his ticket and saved enough to start building a house for their family.

Petar was lucky because the big port was just hours away. Most people, they heard, had to travel for days to reach it. The next best port would have been Trieste, or Genoa in Italy. But Fiume already had a direct biweekly line to New York and the Cunard Steamship Company had just introduced a third steamship. Besides, the United States had just opened a consulate in town and the first job of Fiorello La Guardia, a consular official and the future mayor of New York, was to take care of the emigrants. He had spent two years in Fiume and even learned the Croatian language. This meant that all the necessary formalities were done there, in the port, before embarking on the ten-day trip.

The end of the nineteenth century and the beginning of the twentieth was a time of mass emigration from Europe to the United States: tens of millions of people from Eastern and Central Europe traveled from northern European ports like Hamburg or Bremen, or from southern ones like Genoa and Fiume, then ranked eighth in terms of the numbers of sea passengers departing from there. According to some estimates, half a million Croats immigrated to America during this period. In Eastern Europe, only Poland and Slovakia could claim to have seen the departure of more emigrants. Poverty drove 55 million Europeans from the continent. Whole regions were emptied out, forcing governments to try to prevent what was then called "American fever." Most remained on the other side of the Atlantic. Petar was part of the same, huge emigration wave. However, my great-grandfather returned and built a house. He also brought with him fine porcelain and clothes, packed in heavy wooden boxes, some of which survive to this day. I still have a small, eggshell-thin teacup that he bought in Little Italy in New York City, where he lived. Antonia was pleased, as the bad times were behind them. Forever, she believed—but in fact World War I was just a few years away.

After six decades and yet another world war, the late sixties and early seventies were a time for another wave of mass emigration. From the same territory but not the same state. Now citizens of the Socialist Federal Republic of Yugoslavia departed for Sweden and Germany. Around a million people left on buses and trains to become temporary guest workers, or *Gastarbeiter*. This resulted from an extraordinary measure taken by the communist government to cover up the failure of the planned economy. The money these workers sent home kept their families and the whole country going for quite a while.

In return, Yugoslavia opened up the country to German tourists—despite the fact that we had learned to hate Germans, because they were the enemy in World War II; there was even a town where they were forbidden to visit. But suddenly they were okay. Every summer more and more of them came to the fishing villages and beaches, and local kids were supposed to be nice to them and not laugh at their funny habit of walking in the sea with plastic shoes on. They brought money, deutsche marks, or DM. Soon DM became an informal local currency. If you wanted to buy a car, an apartment or land, you would pay in DM. How was that possible in the country where there was no legal way to exchange the local currency, the dinar, into DM? This was one of many mysteries of life under the specific Yugoslav type of communism.

Many children grew up largely without their fathers, who would visit only twice a year, for the Christmas and Easter holidays. My classmate Vera grew up like that, though her father was among the first to start building a new house in his seaside village. It consisted at first of only one floor, but every few years another floor was added, until the three-story house became the biggest in the neighborhood. An ugly cement construction, self-built without permission or an architect's plan, without façades, the two upper floors unfinished—but still the biggest. Vera's father drove a white Mercedes, secondhand to be sure, but nobody else had such a car back then. She got a bicycle we could only dream of and her family was the first to have a color TV set. . . . But growing up without a father was the price she paid.

When he returned for good, he was an old man and his daughter was already married, living on the first floor of the house he built. The second floor was, of course, rented to German tourists.

None of my relatives left in the seventies. People from the islands or the Adriatic coast no longer left to find a job far away. They lived well as more and more tourists visited, not only Germans. First the locals would rent a room in their old house, then extend the old house, then build a new house, all the while offering not much more than sun and sea.

Then, because of the breakup of Yugoslavia, the Republic of Croatia became an independent state in 1991. Two decades after independence, it was time for new emigrants, who were also migrants because they moved for economic reasons within the EU. This time they mostly left inland regions with rich soil that used to grow wheat and corn, and where there were farms with pigs and cows. But corrupt privatization schemes and the switch from public to private ownership meant that solid enterprises disappeared, while others had been destroyed in the war during the nineties, and private farming no longer paid off. There were fewer and fewer jobs and people in the region of Croatia stretching from Zagreb toward the east had to move either to towns or abroad in search of work. Ads for houses for sale give a realistic insight into the situation. For example, in the region of Slavonia one could find a house in good condition for seven thousand euros, the price of a second-hand car. In the last eight years, prices have dropped by 50 percent. Only old people remain there now and when they die, the property is usually sold for almost nothing.

The young are leaving because there are no jobs, and if you do not have a job you cannot afford a mortgage, not even for a cheap house. Young people in this part of the world, especially men, live with their parents for lack of money and the opportunity to earn it—no less than 84.6 percent of young people in Croatia. On average, they leave their parents' home when they are thirty-three years old. "There is simply nothing to live on here," says a real estate agent in Đakovo, a small town in Slavonia.

Bus stations in these towns are very crowded on Sunday evenings, especially after the holidays. Buses leave for Germany and Austria daily; there are special charter lines for migrants—or are they *Gastarbeiter* once again? Passengers hug and kiss the family they are about to leave behind; many people are crying. The tearful goodbyes distinguish them from ordinary passengers. The next time they will see each other is Easter.

Many a young wife with small children stands at the bus stop in Vukovar, Slavonski Brod or Osijek, waving goodbye to her husband as he leaves on a bus for Munich, Stuttgart or another German city. Germany is not so far, and there they will stay with a relative or a friend who left previously and has a job at an IT company. Or there is an elderly aunt or a mother saying goodbye to her daughter, a qualified nurse.

Nowadays, according to official statistics, nearly 20 million people of working age (twenty to sixty-four), or about 4 percent of the EU's population, live abroad in another member state, compared with 2.5 percent ten years ago. Among post-communist member countries, the most so-called mobile EU citizens come from Romania (19.7 percent), followed by Lithuania, Croatia, Latvia, Bulgaria, Poland, Slovakia and Hungary. The EU member states where people of working age do not tend to leave are Germany (1.0 percent), the United Kingdom before Brexit (1.1 percent), Sweden and France (both 1.3 percent).

Migration from poor to rich EU member states can be a problem not only for the sending countries but also for the receiving ones. In the United Kingdom, migration from Eastern European countries was, besides sovereignty and identity, probably the most important reason quoted for the "Leave" vote in the Brexit referendum. Immigration and the state of the National Health Service were top concerns for both Conservative and Labour voters, while unemployment and poverty were close to the bottom, unbelievable as that may seem. When a BBC journalist asked a woman of about forty why Great Britain should leave the EU, she did not hesitate: immigrants and national health insurance, she said. By immigrants, she meant migrants from the other member states; in 2013–14 alone, some 560,000 people arrived, with Poles among the top three nationalities. Furthermore, many Britons believe that migrant workers misuse the national health system and take more money in the form of services and benefits than they contribute in taxes. The fact that foreign workers are needed, or that there is data showing they take less money from the state than they contribute to it, means little because beliefs are not based on facts.

In the last 150 years, poverty, hunger, wars and ethnic cleansing caused Eastern Europe to become a territory of emigration. But why should it be so again now, thirty years after the democratic transition commenced in 1989? As soon as EU membership gave citizens of Eastern Europe the right to leave and work in the West, many migrated. The situation is not the same in every country, but the problems are rather similar; corruption, lack of jobs, poor pay, distrust of political elites governed by self-interest instead of governing for the public benefit—these are all common factors, and any difference stems from the degree to which they prevail. The transition period has been harder and less successful than people expected. So far it has taken decades, and many among the generation born at the beginning of the transition are leaving. This generation is not nostalgic like their parents, who were born under communism and who—when confronted with job insecurity in today's economy—can summon the memory of feeling secure under the previous system and romanticize it (although the same cannot be said for the political system). Their children's arguments are not only the usual economic ones, but psychological too. Resignation, depression and apathy reign among these young people because they see no hope for themselves in their own country. Now, there is no longer anything to stop them from establishing themselves abroad.

"Migration is bad," said the Croatian president, Kolinda Grabar-Kitarović, when asked what she thinks about the huge number of Croats leaving the country. She was instantly branded an autocrat who wished to limit freedom of movement. A small country of barely 4 million people that is losing hundreds of thousands among its vital young population is every nationalist's nightmare.

Yet before, the people leaving were peasants and unskilled or low skilled workers; now about one third of them have a higher or university education. To be precise, 32.4 percent of mobile EU citizens have a university diploma. For the first time those leaving are also young professionals: IT specialists, engineers, nurses, lab technicians, chemistry graduates, computer technicians, mechanics, mathematicians, physicists. A degree in the natural sciences gives you a better chance of finding a job. Of course, unskilled workers are leaving too. Nonetheless, Eastern Europe is experiencing the phenomenon of brain drain for the first time.

I recently called a dental clinic to make an appointment with my dentist, only to be informed by a secretary that he is no longer working here. He left for Switzerland. I was a bit surprised because he worked at the biggest private clinic in Croatia, and dentists and nurses are supposedly well paid. But my dentist is young, has a PhD and a specialization, speaks several languages and is not married. I do not think he was motivated to leave for a higher salary alone, but rather to improve his professional status as well. Perhaps the case of Dr. Igor Rudan, a leading researcher in biomedical sciences, could serve as an illustration here too. Having acquired his PhD and specialized in public health, he left for Scotland in pursuit of a second doctorate. After sixteen years, he became chair of international health and molecular medicine at the University of Edinburgh and a fellow of the Royal Society, the first Croat to achieve this since Rudger Boskovic, the famous eighteenth-century physicist, astronomer and mathematician. Asked in an interview about his success abroad, Rudan stressed that he achieved it "without any connections." Merit means little; without such a network of nepotism in Croatia and elsewhere in Eastern Europe, next to nothing can be achieved. When it came to the question as to what might tempt him to return to Croatia, Rudan answered candidly, "Nothing! You simply have no possibilities there for professional development."

But not all educated people have the chance to leave and work abroad in their chosen profession. There are roughly two categories of people who are staying behind: those who have it good and those who have it bad, but simply have to stay. This doesn't mean that, given the chance, the whole population would emigrate, but there are young and middle-aged professionals who remain in the country even if they want to leave. Those who have studied humanities and social science subjects and whose work is directly linked to the language, for example: journalists, teachers, professors, writers, lawyers, actors. They get very few chances to compete for a career in the West, where they are not generally needed unless they are willing to work as waiters, couriers, cleaners, etc. However, their situation at home is precarious too: badly paid temporary jobs are often the norm in their professions.

We all know people with a diploma who are unemployed, who feverishly look at the ads and fill out forms for EU grants for all sorts of activities, who are desperate and tired of searching for some sign of hope that their situation might get better. This too is the same all over Eastern Europe.

Jana is a sociologist from Slovakia with a PhD in feminist history. Last year, her three-year grant supporting her position at the University of Amsterdam expired. During her time there, she published a book in Britain that brought her some international recognition. At thirty-nine, she has moved around the EU continually, from grant to grant, from one short-term project to the next, always hoping to get a steady job. After Amsterdam, Jana spent six months in Vienna, then moved to Budapest on an even shorter grant. She could afford such a life on the move because she has no family. But if she wants to have a child, she has to settle down. Last time I saw her, she told me that she could not go on any longer as she had previously, that she was giving up on writing a new book and on her career in sociology. She is now looking for a job in IT, in which she also has a degree to fall back upon.

On the other hand, there is the case of Katarina, a thirty-six-year-old woman in Zagreb, with a family and a child and a lot of experience with low-paid jobs but no permanent job. She is not considering leaving the country. That would be difficult not only because of the family, but because of her profession. She has a degree in world literature and has published three books. Yet she only ever had temporary jobs, a few months here and there as a lecturer and teacher, replacing someone on sick leave or maternity leave.

"How can I get a proper job when all the ads ask for at least a year of continuous experience in the profession? How am I going to get this experience if all I get is a few months?" she says.

In most cases, when a post becomes available for which she would be qualified, it is already decided in advance who is going to be appointed. More often than not, the advertisement is tailor-made for a cousin or a daughter or an acquaintance of some VIP. The combination of corruption and unemployment led to a new word being coined in the Croatian language: *uhljeb*. There is no literal translation but it means to receive employment through a connection, even if the person is not qualified and the job is useless anyway, and sometimes even if the job is invented just for that person. It is usually some local and insignificant administrative job where the person sits there doing nothing and receives a monthly income. But it could also be an important job in the government, for public television or other institutions. In Croatia, all public administration jobs are referred to using this invented pejorative term, regardless of whether the people doing them are competent or not, much like in communist times, when everybody had to be employed and many useless jobs were created to keep them working. Thanks to this new-old system of employment, the country is experiencing the malign growth of local and state administration. But the effects of corruption in the job market are visible, from the poor performance of schools and hospitals to lousy media and the inefficient legal system. Even in politics, third-rate bureaucrats have finally gotten into power, only to demonstrate their incompetence.

If today all jobs are insecure, those requiring language skills are more insecure than most. And not only in Eastern Europe, to be sure. The thirty-year-old son of my Italian friends in Milan has never been employed. As a journalist, he has only had assignments, and badly paid at that. He has decided to write for free and publish online—and to try to make money some other way. He belongs to the new "precariat" of educated but impoverished young people with an unpredictable and insecure future—the intellectual proletariat, in other words. It is impossible for them to plan their lives at all, and many of them live with their parents, on whom they often rely for financial support. They are not married; they have no children.

In Romania and Bulgaria, educated young professionals started to emigrate as soon as these countries became EU members in 2007. Doctoral students left first on foreign grants, followed by specialists of all kinds, beginning with medical doctors. My old friend Andrei in Bucharest had a heart problem. Some eight years ago he had surgery in the United States. He opted for America and paid for it himself, although he could have received the same treatment in his own country at the expense of the state health-care system, in theory. However, a lack of experts in that particular field made him think twice. No doubt many things have changed and improved with EU membership, but my friend still could not find a specialist in his own country even today. There are simply not enough physicians, because so many have left for other EU countries—some 14,000 in the last ten years, or around half of the total number of physicians in Romania. Of those remaining, four out of five are considering leaving. This is alarming but understandable, as doctors can earn at least triple their monthly Romanian salary in Germany, France, Italy or the United Kingdom. Meanwhile, given that 28,000 nurses left Romania to work abroad during the same period, patients in Romania are right to wonder if any will be left at all before long. The former health minister has said that Romania's health-care system suffers less from lack of finances than from corruption. After all, politics plays a role in whether health professionals receive promotion too. Membership in the right political party can make all the difference—just like old times. In November 2018, the media reported that Romania's finance minister had proposed a "solution": citizens should be given work permits in other EU countries for only a maximum of five years. Although he later modified his statement, there were fierce responses. The business paper *Ziarul Financiar* commented, "It doesn't bode well for Romania that a minister is now proposing a return to the origins of communism. In other words: Comrades, go back to gathering corn and potatoes, the land needs you!" The news website G4 Media has also taken a critical stance on the lack of equal opportunities, inadequate access to education and health care, and the impunity of those in power given the level of generalized corruption. Meanwhile, such "solutions" now tend to be offered by politicians in every country with a high number of mobile EU citizens.

Besides Romania and Croatia, Bulgaria is also among the EU's top labor exporters, according to the European Commission statistics agency Eurostat. In the year 2019, nearly 550,000 Bulgarians lived and worked outside their homeland, 30 percent of them university graduates. The population of Bulgaria is 7 million. In Latvia the situation is no better than in either Bulgaria or Croatia, both in terms of labor shortages and the emigration of educated young people. In all these countries, people respond the same way if you refer to the situation: give us jobs and decent salaries, they say, the opportunity to work in a profession, to have a mortgage, an apartment, a child. . . . We are tired of politics permeating every single aspect of our lives, invading our privacy; we are tired of having our future taken away from us by corruption, lies and incompetence.

Mobility within the EU, a chance to live and work wherever is best for you, is one of the great achievements of the Union. However, small states like Latvia, Croatia and Lithuania are having to deal with serious depopulation; it looks like one day everyone might eventually leave, with the last person switching off the light behind her. Young Italians, Spaniards, Portuguese, etc. are also leaving their countries in great numbers to search for employment. Fewer young people also means an aging population and fewer children—in Croatia in 2019 there were 15,000 more deaths than births—which in turn spells the slow death of the language and culture too. When young people leave their country, they take not only their own future with them, but their country's future as well. And yet when 250,000 mostly young people leave a small country of 4 million citizens, 1 million of whom have already retired, it is not the same loss as when 4 million leave a country of 20 million like Romania, even if the percentage of young people among the migrants is comparable. The consequences are dramatic in both cases and this is cause for concern. But what needs to be done is no mystery, because migration is not new. The answer is universal: creating the conditions for a decent life so the people do not need to leave. The action Croatia took sounds more like a script for a Czech comedy: it created the Ministry for Demography! As if such a ministry would be able to provide jobs, bank credit or apartments, instead of sad statistics. The ministry did manage to recommend a series of proposals, but since longer and fully paid maternity leave, for example, requires a great deal of money, one can be sure that the measures will merely remain on paper. The futility of this "solution" is reminiscent of the Romanian one.

A sorry paradox of nationalist populist governments is that those politicians who shed tears over migration are the same ones who create the conditions for people to leave. They have nothing to offer but promises that their people cannot live on.

If migration within the EU creates such problems, what, then, of the influx of refugees? Could they in fact offer the solution? During the course of 2015 and 2016, a total of almost 2 million people entered the European Union from outside Europe. Most were from Muslim countries, refugees and asylum seekers from the wars in the Middle East.

The loudest opponents of the idea that refugees should be distributed proportionally (i.e., a quota system) among member states were Eastern European politicians, particularly the prime minister of Hungary, Viktor Orbán, followed by other voices from across the Visegrád Group (Poland, the Czech Republic and Slovakia, as well as Hungary) and more. Orbán was the first to reject quotas and justified his decision by expressing fears for the traditional Christian values and culture of his country. He also installed the razor-wire fence along the border with Serbia and Croatia to stop refugees from entering Hungary. At first, this looked like a split between Eastern and Western Europe, because most Western member states morally disapproved of such a drastic measure. But soon they themselves started to strengthen their borders in one way or another. Passport checks were reintroduced and freedom of movement compromised.

For Eastern Europeans, the mere idea that the refugee problem might actually become the solution to labor shortages or depopulation was simply detestable, to the point not only of xenophobia but of racism too. It was not long ago that Yugoslavia fell apart in wars fought for nation-states. Czechoslovakia split into the Czech Republic and Slovakia; Romania still has a problem with its sizable Hungarian and Roma ethnic minorities; even before 1989, Bulgaria tried to turn their Turks into Bulgarians through administrative measures; and Hungarian violence toward its own Roma minority has gone unpunished by the EU for years. The reason for such behavior is the desire to build sovereign and homogeneous nation-states with as few minorities as possible.

They did not finally win their independence from the Soviet bloc, go their separate ways or wage war with their neighbors in order to receive complete strangers. Yet now that they finally have their own states, they are expected to renounce their victimhood and national homogeneity in order to show solidarity. What of the decades spent under communist totalitarian regimes, which had surely made them well qualified as victims entitled to compensation for their suffering (i.e., financial aid from the West)? They were not ready to compete with refugees, most of them from outside of Europe and Muslims, for this status. Some former communist states resisting the wave of Muslim refugees had spent centuries under Turkish—that is, Muslim—rule. They had often fought wars to protect Christian Europe against the Turks, at least as they see it. The wars that broke out in the former Yugoslavia (1991–1995) constitute another recent example of the same thing, of which the ethnic cleansing and at least a million war refugees and displaced persons were part and parcel.

So no, populating Eastern Europe with refugees is not viewed as the solution to emigration and low birth rates among their own people. In his 2019 State of the Nation address, Viktor Orbán said: "We are living in times when fewer and fewer children are being born throughout Europe. People in the West are responding to this with immigration: they say that the shortfall should be made up by immigrants, and then the numbers will be in order. Hungarians see this in a different light. We do not need numbers, but Hungarian children. In our minds, immigration means surrender. If we resign ourselves to the fact that we are unable to sustain ourselves even biologically, by doing so we admit that we are not important even for ourselves. So why would we be important for the world? The fate of such peoples is slow but certain obliteration, until they become a mere cloud of dust on the highway of nations."

Are such words of fierce nationalism enough to stop people from leaving? Faced with new east-to-west migration, with brain drain and general depopulation, Eastern European leaders do not know much better than to lament the fate of their countries, spread fear of immigrants and propose restrictions or benefits that cannot be realized. In doing so, they are denying themselves faster transformation and development. For too many young educated Eastern Europeans, freedom of movement translates into freedom to leave uncertainty behind. And as long as such conditions persist, no patriotic speech can stop them. In yet another paradox, nationalist governments are working against their own declared interest, because it is their citizens who are slowly but surely contributing to the creation of the United States of Europe.

The Tune of the Future

*Italy 2011: Old Europe,
new Europe, changing Europe*

To its citizens Venice is probably at its most beautiful when seen from afar, like in one of Canaletto's eighteenth-century *vedute* paintings. On an autumn afternoon, when its magnificent palaces are reflected in the shimmering water, Venice, in all its unreal beauty, really does look like a movie set.

Indeed Venice today is not much more than a stage setting.

When my first-floor neighbor at the palazzo where I had rented an apartment finally came downstairs, I pulled the heavy front door shut after us. In her late eighties, Signora Immacolata walked with a cane. We headed down Calle dei Fabbri for her to show me the nearest supermarket. Our progress was slow, not only because of her but because at nine o'clock in the morning the street leading from the Rialto Bridge to St. Mark's Square was already packed with tourists. Diminutive and stooped, dressed in black, Signora Immacolata barely managed to make her way through the crowds, dragging her shopping cart behind her. When we reached the first little bridge she stopped. Holding on to the railing, she hardly managed to haul herself onto it.

There are two such bridges crossing the canal on the way to the supermarket and both of them are stepped. Even though the Co-op supermarket near the Campo Santa Maria Formosa is only a leisurely five- or six-minute walk from her house, it takes Signora Immacolata at least twenty minutes to get there. And when we arrive we find a long line at the checkout counter; it seems every budget-conscious tourist had already found their way here. All in all, it takes the old lady at least an hour to do her shopping. "And it's like that every day," she sighs. Her legs are still okay but she cannot carry things up the stairs. Luckily, her *badante*, the Croatian woman who looks after her, is due back soon.

There used to be a bakery near her apartment in Corte Gragolina, and little general stores, and a butcher and a greengrocer, and a newsstand, and a cobbler—everything needed for everyday life was close at hand. Now they have all been transformed into souvenir shops. Her street is a continuous succession of small shops selling fake Murano glass, pizzerias charging a fortune for a slice, tourist restaurants, bars and pastry shops. That entire area around St. Mark's Square has only two supermarkets, one smaller than the other, and, I think, a single post office, which I had a hard time finding.

"Venice is not a city you can live in normally anymore," says another neighbor, a bank clerk who lives in the building across from ours. "You can't make it to work or to an appointment on time in the morning because it's so crowded that somebody my age simply can't push his way onto a small boat, *vaporetto*. The whole infrastructure is geared toward tourists, from the prices in stores and restaurants to the theater performances in English and concerts of classical music in churches where the musicians wear baroque costume. Property is absurdly expensive, and there are fewer and fewer supermarkets, schools, kindergartens, clinics, hospitals."

My neighbor is right, of course. In the past fifty or so years Venice has lost 65 percent of its population and only 23 percent, mostly older people, live in the city's historic center. Just a few decades ago, 150,000 people lived in the old part of town, but today that number is barely 40,000, and it is steadily declining: partly because Venice is too expensive to live in and people are moving to outlying areas—to Mestre, for instance—and partly because there is no work for the young and educated. Venice has an excellent university; many young people come here to study, but they don't stay.

"If you don't want to be a waiter or a maid or to help the elderly, you don't have much of a choice. And even those jobs have been taken by foreigners, by immigrants," says the neighbor resignedly.

Still, there's no need to shed a tear for the Venetians. Some are earning a pretty penny from renting out apartments, others have sold their property and are now nibbling away at their capital. The fact remains, however, that for those who live here—and it is an aging population—life is becoming increasingly hard. One has to survive the onslaught of millions of tourists every year, that mass of people pouring through the streets of this magnificent city of canals and little alleyways that are rarely more than three or four meters wide. Venetians know only too well that they are living not in a city—but in a museum. And that Venice is becoming less and less a real, living city, and more and more a museum of Europe's past, embodying all the glory, wealth, power, beauty and art of times long past. That is precisely why millions of tourists come to see it. The mass tourism industry was the first to realize that there was money to be made out of not only the splendor of Venice but also its importance as an open-air museum.

Yet at the same time, the Venice of today is a perfect metaphor for Europe as it once was, the Europe whose culture and values Europeans swear by, take pride in and wish to preserve.

Bari, in the far south of Italy, offers a very different picture from Venice. It is still warm. It is the end of September, but the holiday-makers have gone. On a Sunday evening in the Piazza del Ferra-rese in the old part of town, the incidental tourist will find the locals perched on a low wall or sitting in little cafés drinking beer or strolling around the square, which serves as a kind of *corso*, a promenade. Many people gathered in the square look as if they all know one another. Children are playing tag at nine o'clock in the evening, teenagers are cooling themselves off with an ice cream and their nicely dressed parents, and even grandparents, are stand-ing around talking loudly, gesticulating, like in one of Vittorio De Sica's black-and-white movies from the 1960s. This is a lively town. If Venice is where old Europe is dying, then Bari is where new Europe is emerging. It is one of the entry points for immigrants to Europe.

In the summer of 1991, an Albanian freighter called the *Vlora* sailed into the port of Bari carrying more than twenty thousand refugees. Older readers will probably remember that Albanian exodus across the Adriatic Sea, prior to their "velvet revolution," if the Albanians ever had one. A picture of the huge freighter crammed with people made the rounds of the world at the time. Sometimes, a single photograph can symbolize a particular time or a historical event. So it was with Jeff Widener's photograph of a lone man facing a column of tanks in Tiananmen Square. And with Nick Ut's picture of the little naked Vietnamese girl and her brothers scorched by napalm, with Eddie Adams's photograph of a police chief in Saigon shooting dead a Vietcong with his pistol, and with the recent photo of prisoners being tortured at Abu Ghraib. And so it is with Luca Turi's famous photograph of the *Vlora*. An exhibition of his work, "Flight of the Eagles," had just opened in the foyer of Bari's Teatro Petruzzelli that September.

In that iconic photo, which was on view as part of the exhibit, as the *Vlora* sails in, people throng the decks and railings, clusters of human beings hang from the smokestack, from the ropes, from the masts. In the next picture, they are within reach of the shore and are jumping into the water, swimming, as if afraid that the land will slip from their grasp. And then there is a superb but terrifying photograph of a vast mass of people, taken from above, already disembarked and on the waterfront, standing under the scorching sun. This scene of twenty thousand people frozen just at the moment when they have finally made it onto dry land looks dramatic, biblical.

Those years saw a wave of some hundred thousand Albanians enter Italy. Today their number stands at about half a million. Since Romania joined the European Union, there has also been an incoming wave of almost a million Romanians. Roughly 10 percent of the Romanians are said to be Roma, the scapegoats of Europe's anti-immigration policy. The West deports them and revokes their residence permits (Italy, France), while in Slovakia, the Czech Republic and Hungary they are fenced into ghettos, beaten up and even murdered.

And yet less than a decade ago, foreigners in Italy, and indeed in Europe, did not pose the problem they do today. Anti-immigration, and in particular anti-Muslim, hysteria intensified after the publication of controversial caricatures of the prophet Muhammad in 2005, assuming serious proportions with the onset of the recession in 2008. The people of Bari were supportive and helpful, because at the end of the nineteenth century millions of Italy's poor emigrated from the city and from the surrounding region of Puglia to America, the promised land, where in a matter of two or three generations they became completely assimilated. Some hundred years later, Italy had become the promised land to some other immigrants.

Of late, Bari has served as a transit town for immigrants, more for refugees than for economic immigrants. Accommodated near the airport, they are part of the latest wave of some forty thousand refugees who have reached the island of Lampedusa from Tunisia and Libya, following the political upheavals there. The authorities house the new immigrants in one of the Reception Centers for Asylum Seekers (known by their Italian acronym, CARA) and then a commission decides on their fate. Italy has eight such CARA centers, thirteen Centers for Identification and Expulsion (CIE) and seven First Asylum and Identification Centers (CPSA), with only a few commissions deciding the future of these people. Long before the refugee crisis in 2015–16, Bari was cast into the public eye because of the refugees—more precisely, the asylum seekers from CIE. At the beginning of August, hundreds took to the streets on the outskirts of town, stopping trains and clashing with the police. The result was eighty people injured and twenty-nine arrests.

I ask my new acquaintances about the incident. Every day at lunchtime they gather at Il Borghese, a bar on the corner of Via de Rossi and Corso Vittorio Emanuele: lawyers Dario Belluccio and

Maria Pia Vigilante from Giraffe, an organization that gives legal advice to immigrants; Maddalena Tulanti, the editor of the local paper *Corriere del Mezzogiorno*; social worker Silvana Serini; Erminia Rizzi from the local Immigrants Advice Bureau. This is a particularly difficult problem, says Dario, a human rights activist and one of the few people to have access to the CIE, which is off-limits to both lawyers and journalists. When the Libyans arrived, they came with a smaller number of people from Ghana, Nigeria, Mali, Burkina Faso and other African countries, who had been working and living in Libya for years. Under the law, they are not entitled to war refugee status like the Libyans, but are treated according to their country of origin, regardless of how long they may have lived and worked in Libya. They therefore have no chance of obtaining a temporary residence permit on humanitarian grounds. Not only do their cases take agonizingly long to resolve, but in the meantime the authorities are treating them like common criminals. Deprived of contact with the outside, their living conditions are worse than prison, says Dario. By taking to the street, they were trying to draw attention to their impossible situation.

Among the refugees in Lampedusa are a large number of children. Silvana looks after unaccompanied minors—in other words, parentless child refugees. She tells me about two brothers, war refugees from Afghanistan, who came as teenagers. They were illiterate but now are finishing school and working, she says proudly. Then she takes out the latest issue of the weekly *L'Espresso*; in it there is a report by Fabrizio Gatti entitled "A Children's Prison," about 225 children and adolescents imprisoned for months on end, housed with adults at the CPSA camp in Lampedusa. They live in squalid conditions, without even minimum care, even though these are traumatized children, some of whom have not only witnessed the violent deaths of their parents but also have gone hungry and thirsty for days. In the six months between March and the end of August 2011, 707 children landed on this island, some of them mere toddlers or infants, while others were born on Lampedusa itself. Their situation is even worse and even more uncertain.

Don Angelo, a priest at the church of San Sabino (next to the city beach of Pane e Pomadoro), has the best address in town when refugees need to get help, I'm told. He had just graduated from the seminary when the Albanians disembarked; he saw them on the waterfront and in the stadium, where ten thousand people were detained. The authorities released them only after the intervention of Don Tonino (Antonio Bello, a well-known pacifist and bishop). Don Angelo had also been on humanitarian missions during the wars in Bosnia and Kosovo.

This tall man with red hair and a disarming smile talks about "institutional racism" and about the reasons for the frustration of the rioters, who feel that they are utterly discriminated against compared with the Libyans and Tunisians, even in terms of the color of their skin. He confirms Dario's assessment that they live in impossible conditions, in complete uncertainty as to the length and outcome of the legal procedure to which they are subject. "Their anger is contagious; it will spread to other centers. This is no longer a situation where immigrants gratefully accept a crust of bread, and then keep quiet and wait. They want an answer." Indeed, even before Bari, embittered by the way the authorities were treating them, immigrants protested in Mineo, then in Crotone, also in the north of Italy.

"It's about despair, not some externally orchestrated revolt. It's incredible that the authorities don't see that," Don Angelo tells me.

The gulf between the refugees and the authorities is one side of the coin, but a gulf has also emerged between the locals and the refugees. The inhabitants of Lampedusa, which is closer to Tunisia than it is to Sicily and has a population of just over five thousand, initially pulled drowning people out of the sea, saving hundreds of lives, and helping refugees to survive. But in 2010, by which time no fewer than forty thousand refugees had come onto the island, things went sour. The locals turned against the refugees when the latter set fire to the CPSA, where about one thousand refugees were accommodated (far more than this First Asylum Center's actual capacity).

They were hoping to force the authorities to speed up the resolution of their status; some twenty people were injured in clashes with the police.

The fact is that the government is too slow in keeping its promise to either transfer them onto the mainland or deport them; and so, after the rioting, the mayor declared that he would not let one more refugee onto the island. As a result, this isolated, neglected island became a kind of victim itself, a hostage to the authorities' machinations. Because something had to have gone very wrong for the locals to switch from solidarity to disgust in a matter of a few months. Lampedusans had been the first to reach out and rescue hundreds of drowning refugees, and now they were hurling stones at them, shouting, "Throw them back into the sea. They're all criminals!"

Clearly this small island community, which lives in difficult conditions itself, cannot carry such a heavy burden without help from the state.

Emanuele Crialese's film *Terraferma* (*Dry Land*), which won a special prize at the 2011 Venice Film Festival, is about precisely this clash between humane principles and the law after a group of refugees arrive on just such a small, unnamed island. I saw it in Bari a day after it had premiered. There were only ten of us in the audience at an early evening showing. Maybe it was too early for the movies, maybe it was too hot. Or maybe the audience was so small because of the topic at hand.

The island where the film takes place is inhabited by fishermen. But since they can't make a living from fishing alone, in the summer they live off tourism. When the sea disgorges the first refugees from North Africa onto their island, it complicates their lives, corrodes family relationships and raises moral dilemmas. The refugees are not only a "bad advertisement" for this little tourist paradise, but they bring the kind of problems the locals are unused to and cannot understand. One fisherman puts it this way: "Can it be that the state is prohibiting us from rescuing people from the sea? All our lives we've done just the opposite, and if this is how it is now, then our ways are above this law."

"A beautiful, very humane movie," an older gentleman unexpectedly remarked to me as we were leaving the movie theater.

There were several films on the subject at Mostra, the film festival in Venice, that year, films like Andrea Segre's *Shun Li and the Poet*, Francesco Patierno's *Things from Another World* and the great Italian director Ermanno Olmi's *The Cardboard Village*. Much is also being written about the problems of immigrants and refugees, not only by well-known commentators but also by sociologists, political scientists and writers like Gabriele del Grande and Luca Rastello, to name just two. But the refugees themselves, those who have stayed on in Italy, are also writing. People like Elvira Mujcic, originally from Bosnia, and Igiaba Scego, whose parents are from Somalia. In Italy, there seems to be far greater social and especially artistic awareness of the refugees and immigrants than is to be found in the official policy.

Many people in Italy still remember the exodus that ravished whole swaths of the country, especially at the start of the twentieth century. Italians know that few people leave their country, culture and language for the sake of pure adventurism. They emigrate out of brute necessity—usually to escape war or economic poverty—prepared to risk even their own lives as they set off into the unknown, very much like today's North African newcomers. In the past 150 years, eighteen million people have emigrated from Italy, a figure equivalent to the population of a medium-sized European country. More than five million of them went to the United States, which far exceeds, say, the number of Irish emigrants to America.

Visiting the Museum of Italian Emigration in Rome, I saw why documenting emigration (and immigration) is important for the history of a nation, and for understanding its underlying reasons. Located to the side of the Victor Emmanuel II Monument, on the Piazza Dell'ara Coeli, the entrance to the museum is inconspicuous, certainly not a place where you will see swarms of tourists. No, mostly it's Italians you see here, walking around, looking at the video archive, the library, the rooms exhibiting frayed suitcases and yellowed shipping charts, with passenger lists and identity cards and passports, faded photographs from home, and the first photographs of arrival in their new, faraway countries and continents. Perhaps these visitors are remembering their ancestors, perhaps they are looking for their names on the lists. Letters, diaries, sports clubs, folklore groups—they all tell individual stories of the despair and hopes of these impoverished peasants, who left the south for an unknown world, on their own, some barely fourteen years old. Just like the desperate of today. This was all just a few generations ago; there are still people who talk in front of the camera about the drama of leaving, about parents or other relatives standing on the pier, waving until they become mere dots on the horizon.

As I walked around the museum, I thought of the Haus am Checkpoint Charlie in Berlin. There you can see the many different ways that the East Germans tried to escape to West Berlin, ringed by a 140-kilometer-long wall. Some of these attempts were quite incredible, from flying in a balloon to digging a tunnel under the Wall, from smuggling people in the trunk of a car to swimming the Baltic straits.

At the beginning of the movie *Terraferma*, a flimsy overcrowded boat sinks and all that is left floating on the water are letters, photographs, documents, toothbrushes. Shouldn't such items be collected as symbols of identity and exhibited in a similar museum dedicated to the refugees of North Africa? Shouldn't it collect testimonies to the ordeals of those who suffocated on deck, who drank urine just to survive, who threw living people over the railings? That, of course, would be a museum dedicated to suffering. But it is something the refugees deserve, wherever they may come from.

So I was glad when, not even a week later, I spotted a small news item in an Italian newspaper: "Pieces of wood, family photographs, pages from the Quran, shoes, food boxes, music cassettes . . . items salvaged from the sea or left behind on the boats that carry thousands of immigrants across the Mediterranean every year, all this can be found in a small room, ten square meters in size, which forms the heart of the museum of immigration set up in Lampedusa by volunteers of the Askavusa Association." The endeavor was founded by artist Giacomo Sferlazzo in the hope that others would join the initiative.

You can also find immigration figures at the Museum of Italian Emigration. Italy has 3.9 million immigrants, accounting for 6.5 percent of the population. Caritas Migrantes gives different figures: roughly 5 million immigrants, or 7 percent of the population. Interestingly—and this was confirmed by many of the people I met—Islamophobia is not prevalent here and fear of Muslims is not used as a means of propaganda as it is in the north of the continent. However, activists like Don Angelo and some journalists caution that a different kind of generalization is at work—both the law and the media criminalize refugees as a group. By and large, the authorities treat them like common criminals, even though they have done nothing to deserve it. This is one of the reasons the refugees are protesting. And even that is a problem, because Europe is still not used to refugees protesting. Europeans expect only gratitude.

Public television plays an especially interesting role in the policy of fear. Citing research conducted by the firm Demos & Pi, the Italian newspaper *La Repubblica* writes that in the first four months of 2011, news about immigrants accounted in Italy for 13.9 percent of news programs on TG1. For the sake of comparison, this figure stands in France at 1.6 percent on France 2 television and in Germany at 0.6 percent on ARD. It is worth noting, however, that Italy was experiencing a so-called invasion of immigrants at the time. All the same, the heavy news coverage did not have a decisive impact on the viewing audience. According to the same source, only 6 percent of Italians cited immigrants as their main concern, compared with 55 percent who cited the cost of living.

"This goes to show how the sense of insecurity is a political and media 'construction,' which introduces and stokes 'fear of others' and increases the already present feeling of insecurity that exists for economic and (un)employment reasons," writes author Ilvo Diamanti.

There are numerous humanitarian and civic organizations, such as Fortress Europe, that advocate for the rights of immigrants and offer them very tangible assistance. These organizations believe that immigrants will keep coming regardless of increasingly restrictive, and even immoral, legislation, and regardless of the walls erected and the other obstacles awaiting them. Where they come from, things are even worse. Immigration policy should, therefore, be rational rather than based on fear, because the only ones to profit from the latter are politicians and parties that promise the impossible. Fear of immigrants is the yeast on which they grow.

In Rome, refugees live behind the Termini train station, in a part of town known as Esquilino. I realized how different Esquilino is from other neighborhoods when I took a walk down Via Carlo Alberto toward the Piazza Vittorio Emanuele. There I saw something that I last saw maybe fifty years ago in Yugoslavia: a street knife grinder. The dark-skinned young man was hunched over a big whetstone, sharpening a knife for a woman leaning against a doorway, smoking, waiting for him to finish. They were speaking in Romanian.

This is where my friend Alessandra lives. Admittedly, you can't see the crowds in Piazza Vittorio Emanuele from the big balcony of her top, fifth-floor apartment. The piazza is ringed with shops selling all and sundry, not that there seem to be many buyers. The shops are mostly owned by Chinese. But as soon as she walks out of her building, Alessandra finds herself surrounded by people from different continents, of different colors, speaking different languages. She took in a little boy named David from Cameroon, but after a few years his mother took him back. Looking at David's photograph on her desk, I think of the difference between Europe and the United States: had he been in America instead of Italy, this same little boy would have become American. In Italy neither he, nor indeed his offspring, will ever be Italian, citizens of Italy. But his white peers, whose parents come from Albania or Bosnia, will become Italian, as will their progeny.

Alessandra is a psychologist and works as a volunteer on projects that help immigrants adjust to and integrate into their new environment, by learning the language, going to school and finding a job. The Fund for the Social Inclusion of Immigrants supports a whole range of these programs and activities. Alessandra shows me a book and DVD called *La meta di me* (*Half of Me*), the product of one project that focused on the second generation, the children of immigrants. There are plenty of such initiatives. Experience tells her that most of this generation will remain in Italy and that they need to be given a chance to become equal citizens as soon as possible. She thinks that immigration policy is all wrong. The law allowing immigrants to be joined by their families has been abolished, so that most economic immigrants and war refugees are young men, who wind up facing a whole slew of problems, from depression to alcoholism, drug addiction and crime. They have no motivation and no goal. Brute survival is not enough of an incentive.

Alessandra referred to something I had heard mentioned before— the experience of Italians in the United States. When you give people an opportunity to establish themselves in a society, they usually take it. To be sure, the American melting pot offers a different model of integration; but equally, says Alessandra, immigration policy should be based on both the principle of solidarity and humaneness and the principle of mutual benefit.

One example of mutual benefit is the young author Elvira Mujcic, who was not even thirteen when she came to Italy as a refugee from Srebrenica. A high school and college graduate, today she is a successful Italian writer—for it is in Italian that she writes. As we lunch on *melanzane alla parmiggianna* in a little restaurant in Via del Boschetto, we talk about identity. She sees no contradiction between her Bosnian origins and the fact that she writes in Italian; indeed, she speaks it better than her mother tongue, which, in the course of our conversation, she periodically apologies for. Identity is not some rigid mold you fall into or not. On the contrary, we talk about how the one, let's say Bosnian, does not rule out the other, Italian. She loves Bosnian food, but she loves the Italian language. She no longer wants to live in her birthplace, and it's not just because there is no work in Bosnia. She feels that she belongs here: this is where she went to school, where she lives and works, where she loves.

Still, it was easier for her to assimilate as a refugee because she is European. It is harder for those around the Piazza Vittorio Emanuele, especially if they come from other cultures and other continents. But even here there are success stories. Take the interesting story of the Orchestra di Piazza Vittorio. Today it is quite well-known, with three albums under its belt, some three hundred concerts worldwide and a documentary film. It embraces musicians from Tunisia, Brazil, Cuba, the United States, Hungary, Ecuador, Argentina, Senegal, India and, of course, Italy—but its composition changes. The orchestra was formed in 2002 by conductor Mario Tronco as part of a project to help save a movie theater called the Apollo.

Even more interesting than the story of the orchestra's formation is the kind of music it plays. In Rome one evening I managed to get a ticket to their premiere of *The Magic Flute* at the Teatro Olimpia. Rome's leftist, progressive elite was in attendance that evening—I recognized a number of well-known public figures—because it was simply an event not to be missed. A casual visitor to the auditorium, who knew nothing about either the orchestra or the opera, would have seen it as part-concert, part-opera. They played a mixture of classical music and ethnomusic, jazz, pop, rap, reggae and mamba. Every so often, in between the Tunisian singer and the solo sections on the Arab lute and African instruments such as the kora, djembe, dumduma and sabara, you could hear excerpts from *The Magic Flute*, such popular arias as "The queen of the night," "Papageno," "Sarastro" and "Pamino." Their mélange of opera was performed in six languages: Arabic, Portuguese, Spanish, German, English and Wolof. Not even the story follows the libretto and the ending came as a complete surprise. Admittedly, this was not a *performance* of the opera. Even the poster warned us that it is an interpretation: "*The Magic Flute* according to the Orchestra di Piazza Vittorio."

Pianist Mario Tronco said that this was not about faithfully performing Mozart's piece: "We took great liberties with the score, we chose only what suits our orchestra. Our performance is full of references to other cultures. Our musicians come from far away, and I don't mean just geographically. Each one of them brings to this opera his or her own culture, own language." Tronco added that while Mozart's opera is about "how it once was," the orchestra's performance was about "how it will one day be." And indeed, that opening night was for me as if the orchestra had cracked open the door to Europe's future. Mozart's music lies at the very heart of what we see as Europe's cultural heritage. Most Europeans would probably like to hear the orchestra give a pitch-perfect performance of the original, because that would be proof of integration. This interpretation/adaptation/improvisation on the theme of Mozart, however well performed and interesting, sounds blasphemous to their ears. But it is more likely that non-European immigrants will also bring something of their own to Europe, and that we will increasingly be faced with a mixture of cultures, be it with Mozart or any other holy of European holies.

This interpretation showed that newcomers from other cultures will not necessarily completely adapt to our dominant culture, which is what they are expected to do. Instead, they will try to adapt the culture they encounter, in all its elements, to their own. And they will do so in both the arts and in life. Statistics will be the decisive factor here: with the number of immigrants from Africa and Asia growing, it may not be that just food, music, fashion and customs will undergo change—European laws may do so too. Yet very few people in Europe will openly say today: Yes, that's true, so what?

It seems that to talk about the integration and assimilation of immigrants (the only two models ever discussed) makes sense only up to a point: just when it concerns newcomers from Europe, say Eastern Europe, such as Albanians or Bosnians—but not when it concerns Roma, who come from the same part of the world but do not share the same culture or history. But what about the non-European immigrants pouring in from the south, via Lampedusa, Sicily, the Spanish coast, and from the east, from Afghanistan via the Turkish–Greek–Bulgarian border, where the largest number come from? Europeans, be they pro or contra immigration, agree on the civilizational bottom line that newcomers, especially from different cultures, must not cross—the emancipation of women, respect for human rights, democracy. But what about art, which, by definition, breaches all boundaries?

Maybe it is better to be aware of how the greats like Mozart, Bach and Beethoven might sound in the future. But also of how many other traditions that we hold dear will change, if they haven't already. Take the production of Murano glass. The little island of Murano, famous for its glass since the end of the thirteenth century, presents a sorry picture today. Most of its factories have closed. The jewelry, figurines, bowls, lamps, paper holders, and stoppers that are sold massively in hundreds of Venice's souvenir shops are made in China. Yes, you get a certificate saying that the necklace you bought is Murano glass, but more likely than not, it is Murano glass *made in China*. The ordinary tourist won't notice the difference or even wonder how the little island he visited the day before, where glass is not mass-produced, can churn out such a vast amount of souvenirs. Or how such a wonderful glass ring or bracelet can cost just a few euros. And most important, how the vast majority of these items are identical, that is mass-produced. Because, on the little island of Murano, no two items made by hand can be the same. That's one distinction; their fine workmanship is the other.

During the time I stayed in Venice, I had a chance to see this for myself in a shop behind my apartment, on the corner of Calle Fiubero. Andrea, who works there, took me to the studio and showed me all sorts of objects, from a paper holder to lovely jewelry. They say it is hard to distinguish the Murano made originals from their Chinese copies. On the internet you can find warnings and information about how to tell the difference, but you can also find advertisements for Murano glass manufactured in China. Of course, this is nonsense, since Murano is the name not just of a certain glassmaking technique, but also of the glass objects made in Murano. Andrea picked up two bracelets. One was of precise, flawless workmanship; the other, I could see with a bit of effort, was a crude, approximate imitation. Mass tourism has led to a demand that Murano cannot meet, even when working at full capacity. And, as Andrea says, the Chinese have neither the same understanding of the original nor any moral dilemmas about producing imitations. But what upset me most was when he compared the *millefiori* pearl necklace made in Murano with the one from China. Because that was when I sadly realized that the necklace I had bought in another shop the previous day was a common fake!

The "danger of invasion," as European politicians are wont to exaggerate, lies not only in the number of immigrants (after all, there are only around 200,000 Chinese in Italy, and roughly 2000 in Venice) but also in the investment of money and buying up of property. Money is much faster in bringing change than the number of immigrants. First the Chinese in Venice bought up small shops and turned them into "Murano" glass souvenir and leather-wear shops. Then they bought bars and restaurants; now they are following up with palazzi, turning them into hotels.

One evening, as I was taking the *vaporetto* no. 2 from Ponte dell'Accademia to the St. Mark's stop on the Riva degli Schiavoni, I noticed that entire sections on this part of the Grand Canal were without light. Huge palaces were steeped in darkness, as if nobody lived there. These are the summer residences of the rich. But among them are also palaces that belong to the city and that the city is selling off, explained a friend of mine who lives here. Change comes in many ways, not just with the poor wretches who make it in one piece to Lampedusa or some other patch of Italian soil; not just through food, fashion, custom and music; but also via banks, investments, money laundering, corruption of the local administration. And while Europeans ponder future changes and whether to put up a wall around Europe (if only they knew what its boundaries were), while they contemplate measures that will contain immigrants at that same imaginary border and Europe's culture and the values that need to be preserved (although globalization—in other words, Americanization—has already utterly changed them), the Chinese are investing, buying palaces in Venice in order to turn them into hotels, thus making even more money out of Europe's cultural treasures. From the Venetian viewpoint, in comparison with the investments of the Chinese, the fear of Muslim immigrants in France and Germany and farther north looks almost pathetic.

My neighbor the bank clerk says that Venice is increasingly turning not into a museum, as I romantically thought, but a Disneylandish amusement park owned by the Chinese, who alone profit from it. He is probably right. Be it at a slow pace or fast, legally or illegally, with or without money, as refugees or otherwise—the immigrants are coming. As I leave Venice with my fake Murano necklace, listening to the Orchestra di Piazza Vittorio, I try to imagine what Mozart would sound like if his music were adapted, not only performed, by a Chinese orchestra in the Teatro La Fenice in the not so distant future.

My Brexit

Whatever the politicians and experts may say, Brexit is a loss for both sides, for the United Kingdom and for the European Union. But, I suspect, the perspective of gains and losses is not the same, depending on whether you look at it from the West or from the East of Europe. And in Eastern Europe, Yugoslavia was somewhat different than other communist countries. We learned the English language at school at an early age, we watched Hollywood movies and, from the mid-1960s on, we could travel abroad freely. British culture did not belong only to the Western world; in many ways it was ours too. Most of all because of its music. In the midsixties, when I was growing up, their rock and pop music became the main bridge between our cultures.

The most popular boy in my freshman class in high school was a certain Zoran. He was neither especially good-looking nor especially smart. But he had that special "something." He had long hair. Not really long, just a bit over his ears. It was called "*bitlsica*" (the Beatles cut) and was modeled, of course, after the four band members of the Beatles. The year was 1964 and it was not a look commonly seen in our country. Teachers did not approve of it because it was considered to be a Western craze; parents did not like it either; and even some of the boys in the class bullied Zoran. I guess they were just jealous that he had the eye of all the girls. Zoran did not care much about what the old people thought, he was playing his electric guitar in a garage band and this was how a guitar player should look.

We were all fifteen then. The Beatles look and Beatles music were our thing.

We could listen to "our" kind of music on the radio. The radio was a magical source of music at a time when most households did not have a record player, that expensive and cumbersome machine for listening to vinyl. I remember that there was a daily program on Radio Zagreb from noon to 1:00 p.m. called "Listeners' Choice," which we always listened to and that's where I heard the Beatles for the first time. Or we would listen to the legendary Radio Luxembourg, which used to air the latest hits. Later, starting in 1968, every Monday evening Radio Belgrade devoted its so-called "First Program" to rock 'n' roll music in Yugoslavia.

This new band on the British and world music scene became a way of communicating, of being one with the world, while at the same time it gave us a sense of individualism, of looking different than our parents. It was more than a style of music, it was a style of life. We saw the photos of John, George, Paul and Ringo in our daily press and on our TV screens. Of course, the phenomenon of a bunch of screaming teenage girls, running after the Beatles wherever they went, was depicted as scandalous and decadent, as the mass hysteria of kids. Perhaps it even was. But such popularity for a band of musicians—Beatlemania, as it was known—was novel to us. We congregated en masse only when we had to—for some state holiday, standing and listening to endless speeches. Or for a soccer match. Big rock concerts had not yet arrived in our neck of the woods.

Soon, however, all the boys were wearing their hair longer, thinking it would make the girls run after them like with the Beatles. In the provinces young men were even beaten up for having long hair and had it forcibly cut off. But that lasted for only a short time, because by the seventies, when I went to college, the fashion and the music had become unstoppable: to be in, a boy had to have long hair, and we girls had to have skirts short enough to wear as a mini, introduced to the world by the British designer Mary Quant around the same time. These skirts were indeed mini, causing our parents much more of a headache than a boy's long hair. It was only when I had a daughter of my own that I could understand their fears. Like many a parent, my father believed that if girls dressed that way, they were more likely to expose themselves to sexual violence and therefore he strictly forbade me from wearing a mini. The problem was easily solved in Yugoslavia, like elsewhere in the world I guess; I would hide my miniskirt in my school bag and change into it later. We wore proper-length skirts to school but the mini was obligatory for going out, to a party or the movies.

It is interesting, if not paradoxical, that most such rock 'n' roll musicians, or "rockers" (as they were called), were the sons of army officers, of the ruling class, the so-called red bourgeoisie. Perhaps they were more privileged and could afford musical instruments and vinyl, travel and be better informed. On the other hand, long hair and foreign music were a clear sign of rebellion against a father's authority. One's look was not as innocent as before—it became a statement.

For us it was perhaps the first notion that fashion could also be a sign of rebellion. For quite a while, long hair was considered if not a political provocation then at least a bad influence. However, as one's look—that is, fashion—was the only sign of "deviation," it was not seen as a threat to the system. Many youngsters in miniskirts and with *bitlsica* haircuts soon became members of the Communist Party. By the end of the sixties the musical *Hair* was staged in Belgrade, the first time ever in a communist country. Deep Purple gave a concert in 1975 and the Rolling Stones in 1976. The explosion of local bands playing Yu-rock , as the local variety of rock 'n' roll was known, was inevitable.

But at the time when I first heard the Beatles, there were no cafés, no clubs, no place for us teenagers to meet, other than dance halls. I had my parents' permission to go because the dancing was organized by the school and it was considered to be more of a dance school, not really an occasion for entertainment. It was a sad place, with benches lined up along one wall, and it was obvious that the dance hall also served as a venue for gymnastic and ballet exercises, Ping-Pong competitions and occasional amateur recital performances. The smell of sweat and floor polish hung in the air. It wasn't much fun sitting there with your back to the cold wall, listening to the crackling sound of vinyl records, under the watchful eye of a teacher worried that we might misbehave in some way, dance too close perhaps. The dancers among us were very few; we did not feel confident enough in our bodies to follow the steps of the waltz or tango; and they didn't play rock music or the twist there. It was some time before rock 'n' roll took over the dance halls, clubs and private parties, allowing our bodies to move in a different way to a very different kind of beat.

One of the important elements in embracing Anglo-Saxon

music, first and foremost rock 'n' roll, was the language. By the age of fifteen, kids in Yugoslavia would have learned basic English at school. A foreign language was obligatory and usually the choice was among English, German and French. In my generation, only a very few chose German, it clashed with what we learned in history class about the role of fascist Germany during World War II. The French group was even smaller; the biggest was English. Some elementary schools had Russian as a subject, but even fewer kids studied that. As TV sets, those bulky boxes with small black-and-white screens, increasingly entered our homes, we were able to watch movies in the original, with subtitles in Serbo-Croatian, as the language was called back then. It was the same when we went to the cinema; all films were shown in their original language and the vast majority were Hollywood movies. This enabled us to get used to the sound of English—although with American pronunciation—and to expand our vocabulary. I remember the good feeling it gave us to listen to and understand the words of Beatles songs. It gave us a sense of self-confidence, even pride. The same was true of Elvis Presley, Chuck Berry or rock 'n' roll in general for those born just a few years before me. But for some reason, for my generation the music of the Beatles, and also the Rolling Stones, meant more. Maybe because it appeared just when we were growing up and we considered it our own. They were exciting in another way too, even if the lyrics were banal and the melody rather simple, like "She loves me, yeah, yeah" or "I can't get no satisfaction." It was a distinctive sound that called for a different kind of dancing. It felt like a sudden rush of excitement filling your whole body, almost like a fever: it made you want to move your limbs.

Perhaps its biggest value was that it was so very different from what we in my country listened to in the sixties. There, music festivals were the most popular way of presenting light music, popular with the wider public. The singers were our first glimpse of stardom, they were our first celebrities. I still remember their names: Ivo Robić, Zdenka Vučković, Vice Vukov, Tereza Kesovija. A music festival was a big event, especially the one in Opatija, a small seaside resort that had been very fashionable among nineteenth-century Austro-Hungarian nobility. At the time when Croatia was a part of that empire, it was known as Abbazia. The festival there started in 1958, organized by Yugoslav Radio and Television, a state institution, and was broadcast live.

It was glitz and glamour the communist way. Women teased their hair, wore heavy makeup, and stood stock-still behind the microphone as if afraid that their elaborate hairdo would collapse if they dared to move to the rhythm of their song. But more exciting were their dresses, worn with very high heels, probably bought in Italy. They were custom-made evening dresses for women, and suits for men, which today only the rich would be able to afford. That was because you could not buy such elegant garments in state-owned stores. Such festivals were as much a fashion event as a musical one. You could see long ball gowns and elegant evening wear in silk, chiffon, satin and organdy. Even if the TVs weren't in color, the impact was great. Women copied the gowns and wore them for festive occasions. My mother had one such evening dress made out of black silk, cut tight at the waist, covered with tulle and glittery sequins, with two thin straps to go over her bare shoulders. To me she looked dazzling, like the movie star Ava Gardner. She would wear it for the New Year's Eve party at the Officers' Club where all the men wanted to dance with her—or so she claimed.

Our festivals were modeled after the somewhat older Italian San

Remo song festival of *canzone*, also broadcast live on TV. I first saw it in 1961. We did not have a TV set, so I watched it on a neighbor's small TV, giving a not very sharp picture in black-and-white. It was a magical experience for us children, but also a special kind of socializing. For example, it would have been out of the question for the owner of the TV set not to let his neighbors watch the festival. Some ten to fifteen people would squeeze into the living room, the children sitting on the floor. It was the same when there was a big soccer match; men would come in, filling the room with cheering and thick cigarette smoke—back then everybody smoked at home and at work, on buses and trains, even on airplanes. As with our singers, I still remember the names of the Italian ones: Domenico Modugno, Adriano Celentano, Milva, Gigliola Cinquetti. . . . We listened to them even though not many people understood Italian.

I think that the most important thing about the Beatles for us growing up at that time was that their music was the exact opposite of the dominant festival music we were used to. Not so much in terms of musical style (some of their melodies could pass for a schlager, or light dancing melody), but rather because it became inseparable from their look and the way they played, creating what became their own specific style.

Now it seems as bizarre to be able to listen to the Beatles parallel with the festival in Opatija, as it was to watch Mickey Mouse cartoons or the movie *Casablanca* in the land of comrade Tito. The mixture of the two worlds colored my generation forever, in both good ways and bad. Good, because we enjoyed greater freedoms than our neighbors; bad, because we were sufficiently satisfied with these freedoms not to see beyond them, not to demand more, not to stand up and create a democratic political opposition when it was needed in the late eighties. While the whole of Europe celebrated the 1989 collapse of communism, Yugoslavia was the only European state sliding toward breakup and war. . . .

From the days of the Beatles onward, my relationship with Great Britain was bound to be emotional. Its music became mine, its fashion, its literature and its TV series, as well as its weird, fantastic sense of humor. Everything except its weather and food.

London in the mid- and late sixties was more appealing (the word "cool" was not cool yet) than Paris or even Amsterdam, where young proto-hippie rebels called Provos lived on boats, listened to rock music and probably smoked weed (we did not yet!), which sounded like paradise to a teenager. London was a place of pilgrimage, and everyone who could afford it went to our mecca, bringing back home the latest vinyl. That is, if they survived driving on the left, "wrong" side of the road, the constant drizzle, their funny money that was impossible to figure out. Once back, these people were the soul of every party and object of envy. Let's go and listen to my records was a standard invitation for romance.

I can still recall the face of the policeman at Heathrow Airport looking at my passport the first time I landed there, double-checking a list of non-visa countries. He could not hide his astonishment that visitors from Yugoslavia did not need a visa for a Western country, but maybe I was his first Yugo tourist. Usually the border police of Western nations had difficulty believing that anyone from a communist country would visit their country as mere tourists, suspecting we would look for a way to stay on. But despite all these suspicions, many of us did come for tourism. Nevertheless, besides visiting museums and shopping streets, there was another reason: going to record stores and rock concerts, which were the most important door into the country, its culture and language.

In the meantime, however, my interest had shifted to books. I studied world literature and read many novels in translation. But as soon as I could read them in the original, it became a special pleasure to delve into Jane Austen, Charles Dickens and, later, more contemporary literature. I would first go to Foyles on Charing Cross Road, the oldest and biggest bookstore, there since 1906, and wander among the shelves of books, just enjoying being there. Even now I would know how to walk there blindfolded from the Tottenham Court Road underground station. But after feeling elated, I would be overwhelmed with a sense of sadness: How many of these books could I read in my life? It did not occur to me yet that I probably would not want to read most of them anyway.

I also started to love the very specific kind of British humor. I can't quite remember when it was that I became acquainted with their humor, but most probably not until the late seventies, when on our now color TV sets we could watch series like *Only Fools and Horses*, *Blackadder*, *Keeping Up Appearances* and my favorite *'Allo 'Allo* or the legendary *Monty Python's Flying Circus*. The Balkan kind of humor is often rough, often dark or simple—irony and sarcasm are not at home here, not to mention laughing at ourselves. The surreal streak that runs through *Monty Python* or the way *'Allo 'Allo* laughs at all the warring sides is something else.

After my obligatory Mary Quant period of fashion, I fell in love with another designer—no, not Vivienne Westwood and punk, which should have been my logical choice, I guess. No, it was Laura Ashley—as if in contrast to Quant, whose miniskirt was a sign of opposition, a scandal, a slap in the face until it became an everyday item. While in London, I discovered Laura Ashley's dresses. It must have been in the late seventies or early eighties when her romantic floral patterns became so widely popular. Her dresses were quite simply cut, but the colors were bright and the floral variations were printed on fine cotton, creating a good-girl look, if, perhaps, a bit rustic. To this day I have no better explanation than the fact that such dresses and lively patterns were not available in my country at the time.

But this is not why her flowers stuck in my mind. In a Laura Ashley shop, besides dresses you could also find sheets and bedspreads, curtains and towels, even wallpaper with the same design. The idea of living within such floral walls appealed to me. Years later, on another trip to London in the spring of 1991, I decided to bring the wallpaper back home to Zagreb and redesign my bedroom. That was all fine and well, except it was the wrong moment. I wanted to change the wallpaper when the whole country was about to fall apart. In Croatia, the bloodshed had started just a month or so before, on March 31 that year, during what became known as Bloody Easter. The first victim was a policeman killed in Plitvice National Park, when a busload of policemen went to recapture the territory that rebel Serbian minority citizens had declared autonomous, after Croatia proclaimed independence from Yugoslavia. His name was Josip Jović and he was only one year older than my daughter. At the beginning of every war people still remember the victims' names.

Nevertheless, I brought home the wallpaper a month or so later. That is another thing that happens to you when war starts: you just assume it won't touch you. It must be a defense mechanism, but it is true that, living in Zagreb, we did not fully comprehend that the front line was only some forty-five kilometers away. A half-hour drive from where I finally did put up the Laura Ashley wallpaper. It looked all cheerful and flowery while out there the real killing had started. Was I closing my eyes on purpose? Was it naïveté or a subconscious attempt to fend off evil?

Indeed, while I lay in my small Laura Ashley cocoon, the war did not hurt me, as if her flowers protected me, at least for a short while.

My subsequent visit to London was not under dramatic circumstances. The war was behind me, I had a publisher in London and moved in writers' and journalists' circles. I was interviewed on BBC radio, had readings at the Institute of Contemporary Arts and started to feel more at home. That is how I once wound up staying at a place where another writer had lived while he was in hiding. People suffer and hurt each other in many ways other than war. That writer was Salman Rushdie, who went underground after the Iranian religious leader Ayatollah Khomeini proclaimed a fatwa (ordering his execution) in 1989 because of his "blasphemous" novel *The Satanic Verses*, whereupon any Muslim had the right to take his life. The small studio belonging to his then wife, the novelist Marianne Wiggins, was located on the ground floor in a row of identical white-façade buildings in Notting Hill. When I had met Marianne during my American tour, she kindly offered me her place to stay. The studio had a back door where Rushdie could escape through the gardens. I could imagine both of them under a red baldachin in that bed in the middle of the studio, with its beautiful carpets, unable to fall asleep, listening with apprehension and mortal fear to every sound out in the street. He must have felt like a hunted animal. In the USSR and other communist countries, dissident writers like Osip Mandelstam, Varam Salmov, Aleksandr Solzhenitsyn, Václav Havel and Milan Kundera had been proscribed, exiled, served their sentence in the gulag or even perished. But they were persecuted by the state. In Rushdie's case, virtually any thug had a license to kill him.

Do Brits really want to become small in the big world instead of big in the small world of Europe? As islanders they have their strange ways and habits, a kernel of madness, I think. I know this because my mother is an islander—although from a small island in the Adriatic.

I see that nowadays British writers and public figures are writing letters to Europe, as if their island were already sailing away from the continent, their politicians having exploited the vague feeling of fear and imaginary threat of Europe until it went further than anybody thought possible. Maybe these letters are their way of psychologically preparing for departure, saying goodbye by remembering their visits to the old continent and anticipating their loss. These are love letters, to be sure.

"Dear Europe," J. K. Rowling wrote in a long letter in *The Guardian* on October 26, 2019. "At the time of writing, it's uncertain whether the next generation will enjoy the freedoms we had. Those of us who know exactly how deep a loss that is, are experiencing a vicarious sense of bereavement, on top of our own dismay at the threatened rupture of old ties."

Perhaps it is time for European writers to do the same, to write to "Dear United Kingdom," or more intimately "Dear Britain," and try to create checks and balances in the same way, to see what they have lost, to remember what they had gained. Britain has a great emotional value for me; it is an inseparable part of my youth. The country is no longer in the EU, but all of that will stay with me because Brexit can't take any of it away; it is already part of my identity. The very same goes for Europe. Political and economic ties apart, Europe is not losing Britain. The British and their culture are so much a part of European identity that even when they sailed away, we had the best of them and will continue to do so. No politicians in this world can pull out their threads of the colorful woven fabric of European culture. It is just not possible.

Acknowledgments

Writing is a lonely job. You sit at your desk alone, day after day, month after month. And you need to be alone; you even love it, especially if you are a woman—because we have so many other things to take care of, which makes it all the more difficult to be alone and devote our time to writing. But in the end, you realize that although you wrote it, it is not only your work, your ideas, your input. If it was not for my longtime editor and friend Kathryn Court, and our conversation over coffee one autumn afternoon in Greenwich Village, this book would never have happened. She and her deputy editor, Victoria Savanh, pleasantly surprised me with their enthusiasm. But I still needed to discuss it with my husband, Richard Swartz, and my friend Carl Henrik Fredriksson. Their advice and comments were very inspiring to me. Some friends and acquaintances, like Marci Shore, Muriel Blaive, Ana Miškovska Kajevska, Oksana Zabuzhko and Oksana Forostyna, read the work in progress and helped me too. My assistant, Marija Ott Franolić, and my daughter, Rujana Jeger, offered their useful comments. And I should not forget Benjamin D. Tendler, who helped me with my English. My special thanks to Samuel Abraham, who shared the story of his photo from 1968 and allowed me to include it in my story.

These people contributed to make my book happen and I would like to thank them all cordially.